THE SANCTITY OF SINGLENESS

six months of solitude
the sanctity of singleness
prayers and journal

The Sanctity of Singleness

six months of solitude
the sanctity of singleness
prayers and journal
By
rev. onedia n. gage, ph. d.

The Sanctity of Singleness

God's words

²² But the fruit of the Spirit is love, joy, peace, forbearance, kindness, goodness, faithfulness, ²³ gentleness and self-control. Against such things there is no law.

Galatians 5:22-23

Now for the matters you wrote about: "It is good for a man not to have sexual relations with a woman." ² But since sexual immorality is occurring, each man should have sexual relations with his own wife, and each woman with her own husband.

1 Corinthians 7:1-2

⁹ But if they cannot control themselves, they should marry, for it is better to marry than to burn with passion.

1 Corinthians 7:9

³² I would like you to be free from concern. An unmarried man is concerned about the Lord's affairs—how he can please the Lord. ³⁴ and his interests are divided. An unmarried woman or virgin is concerned about the Lord's affairs: Her aim is to be devoted to the Lord in both body and spirit. But a married woman is concerned about the affairs of this world—how she can please her husband.

1 Corinthians 7:32, 34

dedication

Those who want to be married

Those who just want to be peacefully unmarried

library of congress

Six Months of Solitude

The Sanctity of Singleness Prayers and Journal

All Rights Reserved © 2020

Reverend Onedia N. Gage, Ph. D.

No part of this of book may be reproduced or transmitted in Any form or by any means, graphic, electronic, or mechanical, Including photocopying, recording, taping, or by any Information storage or retrieval system, without the Permission in writing from the publisher.

Purple Ink, Inc. Press

For Information address:
Purple Ink, Inc.
P O Box 300113
Houston, TX 77230

www.purpleink.net ♦ onediagage@purpleink.net

Onedia Gage Ministries

www.onediagage.com ♦ onediagage@onediagage.com

ISBN:

978-1-939119-62-9

Printed in the United States of America

Other Books by

Reverend Onedia N. Gage, Ph. D.

Are You Ready for 9th Grade . . . Again? A Family's Guide to Success
As We Grow Together Daily Devotional for Expectant Couples
As We Grow Together Prayer Journal for Expectant Couples
As We Grow Together Bible Study: Her Workbook
As We Grow Together Bible Study: His Workbook
The Best 40 Days of My Life: A Journey of Spiritual Renewal
The Blue Print: Poetry for the Soul
From Fat to Fit in 90 Days: A Fitness Journal
From Two to One: The Notebook for the Christian Couple
Hannah's Voice: Powerful Lessons in Prayer
Her Story The Legacy of Her Fight: The Bible Study
Her Story The Legacy of Her Fight: The Devotional
Her Story The Legacy of Her Fight: The Legacy Journal
Her Story The Legacy of Her Fight: Prayers and Journal
I Am.: 90 Days of Powerful Words: Affirmation and Advice for Girls
ILY! A Mother Daughter Relationship Workbook
In Her Own Words: Notebook for the Christian Woman
In Purple Ink: Poetry for the Spirit
Intensive Couples Retreat: Her Workbook
Intensive Couples Retreat: His Workbook
Living A Whole Life: Sermons Which Prompt, Provoke and Provide Life
Love Letters to God from a Teenage Girl
The Measure of a Woman: The Details of Her Soul
Nehemiah and His Basketball
Nehemiah and His Big Sister
Nehemiah and His Flag Football Game
Nehemiah and His Football
Nehemiah and His Golf Clubs
Nehemiah and the Bully
Nehemiah and the Busy Day
Nehemiah and the Class Field Trip
Nehemiah and the Hospital Visit
Nehemiah and the Substitute for the Substitute
Nehemiah and the Two Wheels
Nehemiah Found the Mud
Nehemiah Learns to Swim
Nehemiah Reads to Mommy
Nehemiah and the Hot Dog and the Broccoli

THE SANCTITY OF SINGLENESS

Nehemiah Watch Me Add, Subtract, Multiply and Divide
Nehemiah Writes Just Like Mommy
Nehemiah's Family Vacation
Nehemiah's Favorite Teacher Returns to School
Nehemiah's First Day of School
Nehemiah's Sister Moved
The Notebook: For Me, About Me, By Me
The Notebook for the Christian Teen
On This Journey Daily Devotional for Young People
On This Journey Prayer Journal for Young People
On This Journey Prayer Journal for Young People, Vol. 2
One Day More Than We Deserve Prayer Journal for the Growing Christian
Promises, Promises: A Christian Novel
Queen in the Making: 30 Week Bible Study for Teen Girls
Queen in the Making: 30 Week Bible Study for Teen Girls Leader's Guide
There's a Queen Within: A Teen's Journey to Self-Worth
She Spoke Volumes . . . And Then Some
Six Months of Solitude: The Sanctity of Singleness Notebook
Tools for These Times: Timely Sermons for Uncertain Times
With An Anointed Voice: The Power of Prayer
Yielded and Submitted: A Woman's Journey for a Life Dedicated to God
Yielded and Submitted: A Woman's Journey for a Life Dedicated to God An Intimate Study
Yielded and Submitted: A Woman's Journey for a Life Dedicated to God Prayers and Journal

Six Months of Solitude

Dear God,

It is hard to be single! Lord, please help us to survive the judgement rendered by being single. Lord, help us to follow Your will while we are single. Lord, make us mate—worthy and the patience to wait on the mate You are grooming specifically for us.

Lord, forgive me of my sins which commit while single because I want to be married. Forgive me, Lord, for coveting the relationship of others because I do not appreciate this single lifestyle. Lord, help me to focus on You and all that You have called on me to do while in this single season, which seems to be lasting forever.

Lord, purify my thoughts, rectify my spirit, heal my brokenness, and remind me to love authentically those who You let reach me. I know that Your hedge of protection around me is high and I appreciate that. I am grateful that the people who want to harm me and would harm me are not allowed near me—even when I have invited them in but You vetoed my invitation.

Lord, You are my Rock and Redeemer. I know the value of our relationship and I know what happens when I have to choose between You and a man I hope that You sent and just someone that I selected.

Your word says: [31] What, then, shall we say in response to these things? If God is for us, who can be against us? [32] He who did not spare his own Son, but gave him up for us all—how will he not also, along with him, graciously give us all things? [33] Who will bring any charge against those whom God has chosen? It is God who justifies. [34] Who then is the one who condemns? No one. Christ Jesus who died—more than that, who was raised to life—is at the right hand of God and is also interceding for us. [35] Who shall separate us from the love of Christ? Shall trouble or hardship or persecution or famine or nakedness or danger or sword? [36] As it is written: "For your sake we face death all day long; we are considered as sheep to be slaughtered." [37] No, in all these things we are more than conquerors through him who loved us. [38] For I am convinced that neither death nor life, neither angels nor demons, neither the present nor the future, nor any powers,[39] neither height nor depth, nor anything else in all creation, will be able to separate us from the love of God that is in Christ Jesus our Lord.

The Sanctity of Singleness

Lord, thank You for what You keep me from which keeps me from You. I know the value of our relationship. I never want anyone to interrupt that. Whether You ever allow me to marry or not, I will be forever grateful for the gifts You bestow on me, the achievements in my life, the personal relationships I have, and the infinite love You provide.

I love You, Lord. I know that I am not obedient all of the time. I thank You for the Holy Spirit who helps to convict me. Thank You for the words You speak to me!

In Your Service, God,

Onedia

Your Daughter

Dear Whole Single Person,

Well if you just read that prayer, you will notice I switched from us to me. I had to just pray for me—not that I am not praying for you or that you cannot use my prayer for yourself. I hope that you will. We need energy and power to survive this life and all that it requires and demands. My favorite scriptures read: [14] For this reason I kneel before the Father, [15] from whom every family in heaven and on earth derives its name. [16] I pray that out of His glorious riches He may strengthen you with power through His Spirit in your inner being, [17] so that Christ may dwell in your hearts through faith. And I pray that you, being rooted and established in love, [18] may have power, together with all the Lord's holy people, to grasp how wide and long and high and deep is the love of Christ, [19] and to know this love that surpasses knowledge— that you may be filled to the measure of all the fullness of God. [20] Now to Him who is able to do immeasurably more than all we ask or imagine, according to his power that is at work within us, [21] to Him be glory in the church and in Christ Jesus throughout all generations, for ever and ever! Amen.

We are WHOLE people, whether we have a mate or not. We are just what I said in my prayer, more than conquerors and we have the gear to fight the fight we need to endure daily, Ephesians 6:10-18. Stay focused on God. Seek His will. Once you do that, you will stop being bored or tired or anxious or weary or jealous.

Use this time to become the best person you can be for a mate. Use this time to reinvest in your relationship with God. Do the things you have put off for no good reason. Remember the scriptures from the beginning of the book regarding what God says about singles, behavior

and priorities. I am convinced that if we do His will, He will provide our needs. I know that I am working on that personally. You hold in your hand my 43rd published book. I am trying my best not to walk away from the assignments that God has given me. I hope you will do the same.

Spend some authentic time in these prayers and journal. You will need this information later. Marriage is hard work. With no breaks, vacations, or accommodations. You cannot change your mind once married. You need to be ready for you ask for. You need to be secure in what you are currently doing. God has the big glasses on and He is ordering our steps and our paths. I am convinced that He diverts others so that we do not have to make a wrong choice. Listen for God's voice. Look for His Hand in all that you see and do so that you will understand the why behind the activity.

Reach out to speak with me when you need to. We can pray or just answer your questions or just chat. onediagage@onediagage.com or via twitter @onediangage or find me on youtube.com or blogtalkradio.com. I look forward to your success!

In God's Service,

Reverend Onedia N. Gage

Instructions for Use

Pray and Write.

Six Months of Solitude: The Sanctity of Singleness Prayers and Journal was developed to provide you with an avenue of expression. You should respond to the prayers honestly. Feel free to be transparent. You are addressing these scriptures for yourself, not anyone else. You need to address these issues now so that you are equipped for another person within the boundaries of your space. You need to gain clarity so that you can offer it someone else.

Share.

Share or don't share. Completely your choice. I find that when we write our feelings down, they are easier to share and understand.

Save.

Save your own life. We need to get to a point of understanding ourselves so that we can function in a controlled environment. We want to respond when we have thought carefully and considered wisely the consequences of our actions. If we answer these questions honestly for ourselves, then we can be address our issues in a transparent manner, which will give us an understanding of what we need to grow and mature into as a responsible single. Stop sabotaging yourself and your success.

Time.

The time you spend in this journal is for you. Use it selfishly and wisely!

six months of solitude
The sanctity of singleness
prayers and journal

The Sanctity of Singleness

Table of Contents

Letters	9
The Prayers and Journal	21
All About Me	23
All About God	63
All About the Mate	97
Characteristics of a Single Person	129
On Assignment by God	161
Singleness—What to do While Single	195
Appendix	229
Your Testimony	231
Prayer Directions	234
Prayer Request List/Journal	235
Marriage Covenant	239
Marriage Vows	241
Resources	245
Acknowledgements	247
About the Single One	249

The Sanctity of Singleness

the prayers and journal

The Sanctity of Singleness

All About Me

The Sanctity of Singleness

Psalm 139:14

[14] I praise you because I am fearfully and wonderfully made; your works are wonderful, I know that full well.

Lord,

I am fearfully and wonderfully made. Help me, God to remember that when I am complaining about the variety of things that I can seem to find to complain about. Lord, I need to share how much You do for me, care for me, love me, forgive me, and protect me.

I pray that I can own these feelings and I certainly pray that I can show others that I am fearfully made—a life totally dedicated to You, Lord God.

In Jesus' name,

Your Favorite Single Person

Amen.

_____
_____
_____
_____
_____
_____
_____
_____

Genesis 1:26—27

²⁶ Then God said, "Let us make mankind in our image, in our likeness, so that they may rule over the fish in the sea and the birds in the sky, over the livestock and all the wild animals, and over all the creatures that move along the ground."

²⁷ So God created mankind in his own image, in the image of God he created them; male and female he created them.

Father God,

I thank You for the image You have given me. I am grateful for Your image and Your likeness. I know that I do not use Your image wisely or represent You well. I am praying for Your help in this area so that I don't continue to misrepresent You. I really don't know why.

Lord, I need Your help with my image, attitude, disposition, and my behavior. Lord, I pray that I can make You happy one day.

In Jesus' name,

Amen.

_____
_____
_____
_____
_____
_____
_____
_____

The Sanctity of Singleness

Jeremiah 1:5

⁵ "Before I formed you in the womb I knew you,
 before you were born I set you apart;
 I appointed you as a prophet to the nations."

Dear Father,

When I read these words, I shutter. I do not realize that I am Your plan. I am not clear about how You decided to create me and decide the path for the rest of my life. I have done things which does not match that plan. Lord, I have done things that completely sabotaged Your plans for me.

I am sure that I have challenged the idea of who I would become based on who You actually created me to be.

Lord, help me to return to the person You knew before I was formed in my mother's womb.

In Your Son, Jesus' name, I pray.

Amen.

_____
_____
_____
_____
_____
_____
_____
_____

Jeremiah 29:11

[11] For I know the plans I have for you," declares the LORD, "plans to prosper you and not to harm you, plans to give you hope and a future.

Dear Father God,

Thank You for Your plans for me. I apologize for sabotaging them with my own plans. I know that I miss the mark with waiting on Your plans to manifest. Lord, I try to rush Your plans. So Lord, please forgive me for sabotaging Your plans. Thank You for the hope that You prepare for me and the future that You have planned for me.

Lord, I need You to help me to understand that You will never harm me. Lord, I thank You for the areas where You have prospered me. I know that I take what You provide for granted.

In the Mighty name of Jesus,

Amen.

_____

_____

_____

_____

_____

_____

_____

_____

_____

The Sanctity of Singleness

Romans 8:28

²⁸ And we know that in all things God works for the good of those who love him, who have been called according to his purpose.

Lord,

When I first heard these words, I was encouraged. I need those words to continue to encourage me. I have a hard time viewing the struggles and obstacles as a blessing. Thank You for sharing with me why those 'issues' are blessings. There are some things that I do not understand still but I do know that You can do for me what You choose. And You do. I do love You and while my obedience shows no proof of that professed love. I have some examples of times when I know that Your denial of my requests was for my best. Lord, just help me to accept it more willingly.

In the forgiving name of Jesus, I pray.

Amen.

_____
_____
_____
_____
_____
_____
_____
_____
_____
_____

Galatians 5:22—23

²² But the fruit of the Spirit is love, joy, peace, forbearance, kindness, goodness, faithfulness, ²³ gentleness and self-control. Against such things there is no law.

Father God,

Thank You for the fruit of the Spirit. I know that I disappoint You in this area all of the time. Please forgive me for disappointing You.

Lord, help me with these areas so that my life can reflect these elements. I know that it would please You if I possessed these qualities. These characteristics would certainly benefit myself and others.

Help me reach the fruits of the spirit, so I can please You, Lord.

In the complete name of Jesus, I pray.

Amen.

The Sanctity of Singleness

Romans 8:29—30

²⁹ For those God foreknew he also predestined to be conformed to the image of his Son, that he might be the firstborn among many brothers and sisters. ³⁰ And those he predestined, he also called; those he called, he also justified; those he justified, he also glorified.

Father God,

I am out of compliance of Your image! Please forgive. When You planned for me, You knew me and predestined me to be conformed to Your image and the image of Your Son.

Lord, thank You for giving me such an awesome Brother-Friend-Savior!

You predestined me then You called me.

You called me so You justified me. Because You justified me, You glorified me.

And I deserve none of that! So thank You for Your grace and Your mercy, Your Sovereignty and Your love!

In Jesus' name, I pray.

Amen.

_____
_____
_____
_____
_____
_____
_____

Romans 8:37

³⁷ No, in all these things we are more than conquerors through him who loved us.

Jehovah,

For the works You have done in my life, I am grateful.

Because You love me, I am more than a conqueror in all these things, these issues, these obstacles, and these victories. Thank You for the conqueror You have made me. Lord, sometimes I do not act like a conqueror, but rather, a coward because I muse and worry about things, events, and issues which do not belong to me, but things that I should leave at Your alter.

Thank You for making me a conqueror, even though I embarrass You. Thank You for allowing me to exercise my privilege as a conqueror. All that this means and all that You afford me.

In His Holy name, I pray.

Amen.

_____
_____
_____
_____
_____
_____
_____
_____
_____

The Sanctity of Singleness

Philippians 4:13

¹³ I can do all this through him who gives me strength.

Elohim,

When I realize that I can do all that You assigned to me to do because of the strength You have given to me, I am embarrassed. Not the things I decide to do which have nothing to do with the order You have created for me, I am further ashamed.

Daddy, thank You for equipping me to do Your work. Father, thank You for the strength that You provide me. I apologize for misunderstanding the presence of the strength You provide.

Father, I pray to recognize Your strength in me and I pray to use it correctly and wisely.

In Your name, Jesus, I pray.

Amen.

_____

_____

_____

_____

_____

_____

_____

_____

_____

Ephesians 6:10

[10] Finally, be strong in the Lord and in his mighty power.

Lord,

Thank You for Your mighty power and the strength You possess and give to me. Lord, help me to use that strength and power to others who need the same help I need. Lord, help me live so that I reflect Your strength. Lord, help me live so that I can help others recognize Your mighty power.

Lord, I need Your mighty power daily. Sometimes, I do not act like You have any power. I need Your help. Lord, I don't want to succumb to my weaknesses and my issues and my temptations. Lord, I need Your strength so that I can be strong in You.

You come against my situations and my circumstances so that my life is different.

Thank You, Jesus!

Amen.

_____
_____
_____
_____
_____
_____
_____
_____
_____

The Sanctity of Singleness

1 Corinthians 13

⁴ Love is patient, love is kind. It does not envy, it does not boast, it is not proud. ⁵ It does not dishonor others, it is not self-seeking, it is not easily angered, it keeps no record of wrongs. ⁶ Love does not delight in evil but rejoices with the truth. ⁷ It always protects, always trusts, always hopes, always perseveres.

Lord,

You have shown me the definition of love. You have shown me that demonstration of love. You have equipped me to love. You have told me that You are the replenisher of my love to You, myself and others.

Lord, love is so hard for me at times! I need Your help to love all of the time. I love You subjectively—not like You loved me. I want to love You better. I need Your help loving myself because I don't love myself sometimes, even though Your love created me. I am hard on myself and critical of my life and myself.

Lord, I have a hard time loving others because I am insecure and jealous and unsure. I can't love because they hurt me or all that has happened.

Lord, I need Your help to love!

Like Jesus does.

Amen.

_____
_____
_____
_____
_____

Hebrews 11:6

⁶ And without faith it is impossible to please God, because anyone who comes to him must believe that he exists and that he rewards those who earnestly seek him.

Lord,

May my weak faith not be a hinderance to others. Lord, I know that You placed me here as an example, but sometimes I am not a good example of faith. Help me, Lord, to be more faithful. I need to read more, pray more, and I need to seek Your face more.

I will keep You first. Lord, I will love You with faith.

My faith does not represent You well. For that I apologize. I want to please You! I want You pleased with me.

Lord, thank You for helping me to lift my faith.

In Jesus' name, I plead.

Amen.

THE SANCTITY OF SINGLENESS

Ephesians 2:10

[10] For we are God's handiwork, created in Christ Jesus to do good works, which God prepared in advance for us to do.

Lord,

Thank You for giving me something to do—an assignment. I am glad for my work that You created in advance for me to do.

I know that I complain sometimes. Please forgive me for that complaining. Thank You for the gifts that You have given to me to serve You through those You send my way.

Thank You for me being planned in Your creation. I know that some people have been told that they were unintended, a mistake, but I know that it is not true. Offer them Your peace. Thank You for allowing me to share that fact with others.

Thank You again God for making me!

In Jesus' name, I pray.

Amen.

_____

_____

_____

_____

_____

_____

_____

Six Months of Solitude

Matthew 5:3

³"Blessed are the poor in spirit,
 for theirs is the kingdom of heaven.

Dear Father,

When You bless, You don't miss. You bless me. Just because I am Yours—because I belong to You.

There are times when I am embarrassed by my poor spirit but my poor spirit is what keeps me focused on You.

Your blessings and the promises of Your blessings keep my close to You. Sometimes I struggle to stay close to You.

I am praying that my poor spirit does not cause me to give in to sin or to even consider the temptation.

Thank You for protecting and rewarding my poor spirit. May I serve You well.

In Jesus' name.

Amen.

_____
_____
_____
_____
_____
_____
_____

The Sanctity of Singleness

Matthew 5:4

⁴ Blessed are those who mourn,
   for they will be comforted.

Dear Lord,

As I mature, I begin to understand how death factors into Your plan more. I do not like death because I am going to miss the persons who I am losing.

You miss Your creation more than I do. And others report that their work is done, however it does mean that You want them with You.

Please allow Your comfort to overwhelm me. Help me to accept Your provision of comfort. Help me to share Your measure of comfort when others are mourning.

While I mourn, You have reminded me that I cannot mourn without hope.

In Your Son's name, I pray.

Amen.

_____
_____
_____
_____
_____
_____
_____
_____

Matthew 5:5

⁵ Blessed are the meek, for they will inherit the earth.

Dear Lord,

As a child, I looked up the definition of meek so that could better understand this verse. I wanted to know if I was meek, so that I could figure out if I would inherit the Earth. But Lord, You define meek so that I will remember why You have created me.

Meek is the best report card that You lead my life.

Thank You that You remind me that I don't lose anything when I am meek.

I love You. When I am meek, others knew it as well.

In Jesus' name, I pray.

Amen.

THE SANCTITY OF SINGLENESS

Matthew 5:6

⁶ Blessed are those who hunger and thirst for righteousness, for they will be filled.

Dear Father,

I pray that You continue to intervene when I want take the unrighteous in my own hands. I am exhausted with those who take advantage of people and situations and principalities and power.

It is my hope that You stop them more often. Lord, help me to not judge those who reject righteousness.

Forgive me when I am unrighteousness and wrong, evil and dishonest. Forgive me for the sabotage I cause others. Forgive me for the pain and grief I cause others. Forgive me for the way I am honest, but it causes pain to the self-esteem of others.

Help me crave, thirst and hunger for righteousness.

In Jesus' name, I pray.

Amen.

_____
_____
_____
_____
_____
_____
_____
_____

Matthew 5:7

⁷ Blessed are the merciful,
   for they will be shown mercy.

Lord,

How I crave Your mercy! I pray for Your mercy. I am in need of Your mercy; mostly because I keep failing and flailing to keep my life in an order that is reasonable to You.

Lord, forgive me for not being as merciful as I should be, when I should be, as often as I should be, and without any strings attached. Lord, help me to be merciful. Help me to give others who You have assigned to me than the mercy You have given me to give.

Lord, help me to be merciful so that You will be merciful to me.

In the name of Jesus, I pray.

Amen.

The Sanctity of Singleness

Matthew 5:8

⁸ Blessed are the pure in heart,
  for they will see God.

Dear Father,

Please help me to keep a pure heart. Free from malice. Free from deceit. Pure from hurting others with intention. Free from harm and danger. Free from demeaning others. Free from degrading others. And myself.

Please help me to keep my heart pure. It is wayward from time to time. I mean day to day. Hour to hour. Minute to minute. Second to second. My wayward heart causes damage at times to people who do not know that they will be forever changed by my wayward and impure heart.

Please help me to keep my heart pure. Apart from sin. Willing to serve unselfishly. Sharing Your love with others.

I do want to see You and I want to be able to do so without knowing that I was horrible on the way.

In Your Son's, Jesus name, I pray.

Amen.

Matthew 5:9

⁹ Blessed are the peacemakers,
   for they will be called children of God.

Lord,

Help me to be a peacemaker. Lord, I need help making peace between people who are discontent around me. Lord, I also want to make peace between me and others. I know that some people hate me because of You, but I still want them to be peaceful.

Lord, help me to be peaceful with You. I am cantankerous and disobedient. I want Your undivided attention and I get Your attention in unbecoming ways.

Lord, help me to be peaceful. May my peace be authentic, not driven by ill motive.

May the words on my mouth and the meditation of my heart by pleasing unto Your sight, My Rock and Redeemer.

In the name of Jesus, I pray.

Amen.

_____

_____

_____

_____

_____

_____

_____

_____

_____

THE SANCTITY OF SINGLENESS

John 15:1—2

¹"I am the true vine, and my Father is the gardener. ² He cuts off every branch in me that bears no fruit, while every branch that does bear fruit he prunes so that it will be even more fruitful.

Father,

Help me to understand when You will be gardening within my life. As I reflect over these words, I know that I need to be pruned. I know that there are portions of my life and people who have been pruned away from my life.

I know that there are requests which I have made that I will not receive because of this pruning process.

I want to bear fruit for You. I do not want to be an empty fruit tree that would embarrass Your hand. I want to be fruitful, productive, and make You proud.

In Jesus' name, I submit this prayer.

Amen.

_____
_____
_____
_____
_____
_____
_____
_____

John 15:4

⁴ Remain in me, as I also remain in you. No branch can bear fruit by itself; it must remain in the vine. Neither can you bear fruit unless you remain in me.

Dear Lord,

I would say that I will never deny You or leave You, but I already did that recently. I so want to be worthy of Your love, and forgiveness.

In order to be productive, I have to remain with You. Lord, help me! Jesus, stay close to me no matter how I act, respond, and behave.

I want to remain in You. I need You to love and survive.

Lord, help me to recognize the Vine and to remain there.

In the Mighty Name of Jesus, I pray.

Amen.

THE SANCTITY OF SINGLENESS

John 15:5—6

⁵ "I am the vine; you are the branches. If you remain in me and I in you, you will bear much fruit; apart from me you can do nothing. ⁶ If you do not remain in me, you are like a branch that is thrown away and withers; such branches are picked up, thrown into the fire and burned.

Lord,

I already know what happens when I leave You and believe that I can go on my own. I already saw the destruction and damage that I can do while trying to avoid Your presence and supervision. Lord, I cannot continue walking away from You. I do not want to wither and die, be thrown into the fire and burned.

Lord, I so want to be a healthy and full, blooming and productive tree, attached firmly to the Vine, obedient and loving toward the Vine and the Gardner.

Thank You for Your help, dear God.

In the powerful name of Jesus, I ask.

Amen.

_____
_____
_____
_____
_____
_____
_____
_____

John 15:7

⁷ If you remain in me and my words remain in you, ask whatever you wish, and it will be done for you.

Lord,

I will study more so that Your words can remain with me. I crave Your words to stay with me.

I thank You for the ability to ask for anything in Your name and it be given to me.

I know that I ask for some frivolous stuff. I want to ask for what is within Your will and what will help others. I do want some spiritual enlightenment and I just want You to be pleased and proud of me.

I want to experience Your favor because I remain in You and Your words are embodied here as well.

In the Awesome name of Jesus, I pray.

Amen.

The Sanctity of Singleness

John 15:8

⁸ This is to my Father's glory, that you bear much fruit, showing yourselves to be my disciples.

Dear God,

I have two jobs and it looks like that I am not doing either of them well. I want to bring You glory through my behavior. Lord, help!

I want to bring You more glory because of my fruit bearing. Lord, sometimes I reject the opportunity to produce fruit. I should be willing to produce fruit all of the time. Sometimes I take a break. But You never take a break.

I know that You made us disciples. Sometimes I have a problem with my job. I will do better with Your help.

In the wondrous name of Jesus, I pray.

Amen.

_____

_____

_____

_____

_____

_____

_____

_____

_____

John 15:13

¹³ Greater love has no one than this: to lay down one's life for one's friends.

Dear Lord,

When Jesus called me friend, I wept. Jesus died for me. Lord, I know that I may never be asked to do something so grand and humbling, however, I hope and pray to never miss an opportunity to sacrifice for my friends and loved ones.

Father God, when You mandated a tenth of everything, love was not included. You had already told us that love should be done at 100% to You and everything You commanded. Please forgive me for loving selfishly and with a guarded heart. I am embarrassed that I do not love as I should.

Lord, help me to love as You have prescribed: with my whole heart, extravagantly, and without discrimination.

I want to do better.

In Jesus' name, I plead.

Amen.

THE SANCTITY OF SINGLENESS

John 15:16

¹⁶ You did not choose me, but I chose you and appointed you so that you might go and bear fruit—fruit that will last—and so that whatever you ask in my name the Father will give you.

Lord,

When I read these words—realizing that You chose me?! Knowing that You know my faults and secrets, my flaws and indiscretions makes me even more humble. Lord, remind me of Your choosing when I am begging others to accept me, while I am auditioning for their time, and while I could be serving You, but am crafting ways to be sought out and popular. Thank You for choosing me. I am so unworthy. Everything bad and evil thought and deed is stopping me from being great as You have designed. Lord, You chose me!

Forgive me Lord for the times when I don't choose You. I am so sorry. Sometimes, like often, I fail You in bearing fruit. Please help me to fulfill Your will. Please stop me from disappointing You. May my whole person bear the fruit You designed.

Thank You for considering what I ask in Your name as something I may possess.

In Jesus' name, I pray.

Amen.

_____
_____
_____
_____
_____
_____
_____

John 15:18

[18] "If the world hates you, keep in mind that it hated me first.

Lord,

When You say this, I get upset. Because I detest myself for behaving like I hate You. I hate You when I do not obey and do not love and do not keep watch over others assigned to my care or other sins.

Lord, forgive me for whining when they hate me. I do forget that is by design. I forget that sometimes people hate me so that I am not distracted from Your assignment for me. Thank You for reminding me of what I am called to be and do.

Thank You for shielding me from the real situation and story. Thank You for those who You keep away from me. Thank You for causing them fear such that they are afraid to hurt or harm me.

In the name of my Savior, Jesus Christ, I pray.

Amen.

The Sanctity of Singleness

John 15:19

¹⁹ If you belonged to the world, it would love you as its own. As it is, you do not belong to the world, but I have chosen you out of the world. That is why the world hates you.

Lord,

My Lord, my heart lays prostrate before You right now in total submission to You and Your way and Your will.

I know that I do not always act or appear grateful that I belong to You but I am. I am also quite grateful that I do not belong to them. Lord, help me to not ever be there. I don't want to be mean, rude, manipulative, fake, overbearing, haughty, proud, arrogant, and anything else which separates me from You.

Lord, thank You for my being able to love unconditionally and authentic. Thank You for helping me to discern when it is not authentic from others. And thank You for removing me every time it was not; especially when I did not want to leave the relationship. While I have never understood, I am forever grateful.

Finally, thank You for helping me to realize that if it loves me, it can also always change its mind.

In the Powerful name of Jesus, I pray.

Amen.

_____
_____
_____
_____
_____
_____
_____

SIX MONTHS OF SOLITUDE

John 15:20

[20] Remember what I told you: 'A servant is not greater than his master.' If they persecuted me, they will persecute you also. If they obeyed my teaching, they will obey yours also.

Lord,

I am on my face with Your words. I can no longer make any excuses about what happens to me. I cannot any longer think that I am being singled out because I don't want to deal with the work involved with being challenged because I am Your child.

I am sorry for acting like I am too good to be persecuted and that I do not deserve that treatment.

Lord, thank You for reminding me to depend on You in these times, to seek You in these situations, and to believe that You are watching me to make sure that I am following You and Your covenants.

In Jesus' name, I proclaim.

Amen.

The Sanctity of Singleness

John 15:21

²¹ They will treat you this way because of my name, for they do not know the one who sent me.

Father God,

Help me to be strong enough to remember that it is not about me, but about You and Jesus. They are after me because of You and Jesus. I am forgetful that it is not about me.

Lord, I am reminded that I am a target because of You. I know that You will protect me even during this persecution. Lord, teach me to see this situation to its completion. I know that I cannot quit or walk away.

Help me remain faithful to You during this season.

I am grateful to grow during this encounter.

In Jesus' name, I pray.

Amen.

_____
_____
_____
_____
_____
_____
_____
_____
_____
_____

John 3:16

¹⁶ For God so loved the world that he gave his one and only Son, that whoever believes in him shall not perish but have eternal life.

Gracious Father,

I am not greater than who serves me nor am I greater than who I serve. Thank You for the reminder of being a servant—leader. You created me to serve others, even if I am the leader.

Thank You for the example of Jesus. He walked with the disciples. He taught them; He teaches us. He served lunch to over 5000 people. He hosted a lesson on water.

He fed them the Last Supper. Jesus washed the disciples' feet. He prayed for us.

He teaches me that while He came to save, to teach, to serve, and to be humble, even though He has more power and privilege than others. Thank You for helping to keep myself in line with God's will.

In the name of Jesus, I plead.

Amen.

The Sanctity of Singleness

2 Timothy 4:17

¹⁷ But the Lord stood at my side and gave me strength, so that through me the message might be fully proclaimed and all the Gentiles might hear it. And I was delivered from the lion's mouth.

Lord,

Because I am weak

Because I am a quitter

Because I am mean

Because I am a procrastinator

Because I am fickle and indecisive

Because I am doubtful

Because I am fearful

Because I reject love

Because I omit forgiveness

Because I am a sinner

Because I am loved by You

Because I am Your child

You give me strength, strength I don't deserve, strength which I squander and misuse. Thank You for Your provision to do Your will.

In the powerful name of Jesus, I pray.

Amen.

_____

_____

_____

_____

Matthew 5:10

¹⁰ Blessed are those who are persecuted because of righteousness,
for theirs is the kingdom of heaven.

Dear God,

Thank You for offering me the kingdom of Heaven because I am persecuted for my righteous deeds and behavior.

I needed some encouragement for this matter. I don't deserve this encouragement but I need it. I am sure that I don't know why I am persecuted—exactly what am I doing for You that gets the attention of these who will voluntarily persecute, ridicule, and taunt me? But God thank You for Your provision of comfort during these encounters.

In His mighty name, I pray.

Amen.

The Sanctity of Singleness

Matthew 5:11

¹¹ "Blessed are you when people insult you, persecute you and falsely say all kinds of evil against you because of me.

Dear God,

Oh I need Your help in this! I can tell You that I am not good at extending grace to those who attempt to hurt and harm me. Those who insult me and persecute me. I cannot overlook this matter without Your help.

That persecution makes us hard to continue to share my goodness and righteousness with others. I didn't have these issues when no one knew what I would do for You through others. It was hard enough to do the right thing and to be righteous, but then it was the obstacles which make it difficult to keep doing the right.

God, I know that Jesus did it. I know I should be able to as well. I need Your help. I don't forgive well either.

I want to enjoy Your blessings, so I want to follow Your will.

In Your Son, Jesus' name, I pray.

Amen.

_____
_____
_____
_____
_____
_____
_____
_____

Matthew 5:13

[13] "You are the salt of the earth. But if the salt loses its saltiness, how can it be made salty again? It is no longer good for anything, except to be thrown out and trampled underfoot.

Lord,

Keep me seasoned and flavorful. I need it. I want to please You. The salt You have blessed me with to love others, help others, teach others, be taught, share hope and inspiration, and all that You have gifted me with.

I don't want to underappreciate Your investment in me. May nothing return void that You have placed within me! I want to be among Your choice selections when giving blessings, bestowing gifts, and assigning work.

I never want to be labeled good for nothing.

It is in Your name, Jesus, that I pray.

Amen.

_____
_____
_____
_____
_____
_____
_____
_____
_____
_____

The Sanctity of Singleness

Matthew 15:14—16

¹⁴ "You are the light of the world. A town built on a hill cannot be hidden. ¹⁵ Neither do people light a lamp and put it under a bowl. Instead they put it on its stand, and it gives light to everyone in the house. ¹⁶ In the same way, let your light shine before others, that they may see your good deeds and glorify your Father in heaven.

Lord,

When You said let there be light in the creation of the world, I did not consider that the light included me. You created me to be light.

I forget that often. You built me on a hill. You meant for me to shine, and not live under a bowl—one I created for myself or the one others created for me.

Lord, thank You for empowering me and giving me the courage to stand before others with my gift of Your light in my life. My work, my light, and my life is to glorify. I apologize for needing so many reminders. I apologize for disappointing You so frequently.

Thank You for the light and may I continue to draw all persons unto You.

In the name of Jesus, I pray.

Amen.

_____

_____

_____

_____

_____

_____

Six Months of Solitude

All About God

The Sanctity of Singleness

John 1:1

In the beginning was the Word, and the Word was with God, and the Word was God.

Lord,

When I am clear about the fact that You had our total existence planned for all of eternity, I blush.

So to know that You planned the birth, torture, death, burial, and resurrection of Christ, I am overwhelmed.

I am certain that I don't deserve anything but thank You for everything, especially the plans that You have for me.

From the beginning, I was planned. I arrived in Your timing. I know that I owe a debt that I cannot pay but I am grateful for it all.

In the name of Jesus, I pray.

Amen.

_____
_____
_____
_____
_____
_____
_____
_____
_____
_____

Psalm 8:1

¹ LORD, our Lord,
   how majestic is your name in all the earth!

You have set your glory
   in the heavens.

Dear God,

Oh Lord, my Lord. How excellent is thy name in all the Earth!

When I pray that to You Lord, I am humbled. I enter our special place of communion when I utter those words. Thank You, Lord for being excellent. When David penned these words, he knew what these words would mean to me because of what they meant to him.

There is nowhere that we don't agree on Your excellence dear Father.

I am the child that You made who needs a demonstration and accountability of excellence. I thank You for such a demonstration.

I love You.

In Your Son's name, I pray.

Amen.

_____

_____

_____

_____

_____

_____

_____

The Sanctity of Singleness

Deuteronomy 6:5

⁵ Love the LORD your God with all your heart and with all your soul and with all your strength.

Dear Father,

If only I could obey like I say that I love You!

I really try to love You with all of my heart—in all of its pieces and with all of its impurities, I love You.

Even when my mind wants to stray away from You, I settle on You. When I think of ways to do wrong, I stay thinking about You and Your will for my life.

With my inner most being—my soul—I love You! This broken, malfunctioning soul belongs to You. I am working on sabotaging Your plan for my wholeness, so that I can love without excuse.

In the name of Jesus, I pray.

Amen.

_____
_____
_____
_____
_____
_____
_____
_____
_____
_____

Romans 8:31

[31] What, then, shall we say in response to these things? If God is for us, who can be against us?

Lord,

I am grateful that You are on my side. I have lots of people against me. I cannot depend on anyone by You, God. Even when I think I can depend on others, they fail and betray me still.

Lord, thank You for being on my side and in my corner. I need Your help, guidance, and support during these tough seasons.

I am proud that You are my God in whom I can trust and upon whom I can depend.

Lord, please keep the hedge of protection around me very high so that my enemies cannot attack me.

Thank You God. In Jesus' name, I pray.

Amen.

_____
_____
_____
_____
_____
_____
_____
_____
_____

The Sanctity of Singleness

Romans 8:32

³² He who did not spare his own Son, but gave him up for us all—how will he not also, along with him, graciously give us all things?

Father God,

You are gracious! You are awesome! You are genius! Thank You for Your Son, whom You could have spared in the pardon of my sins. You could have left me to fend for and defend myself.

But You did not! Then You gave me the desires of my heart according to Your will.

Lord, thank You for forgiving me all that You do so that I will be comfortable.

Thank You for the knowledge and the Spirit of discernment that You give to me. Thank You for Your grace and mercy. Thank You for Your forgiveness. Thank You for Your abounding love.

Father God, thank You for Your Sovereignty!

In the name of Jesus, I pray.

Amen.

Romans 8:38—39

³⁸ For I am convinced that neither death nor life, neither angels nor demons, neither the present nor the future, nor any powers, ³⁹ neither height nor depth, nor anything else in all creation, will be able to separate us from the love of God that is in Christ Jesus our Lord.

Father God,

I am not always conscious of the idea that they reason that I do not have certain things or that certain people are not in my life is because they or that 'thing' would stop me from having a solid relationship with You.

I have to be reminded that those things that separate us will not be able to exist in my life.

Thank You for helping me to remember that. Thank You for helping me to see that and realize that.

Thank You for helping to recognize the importance of our relationship and to keep it maintained and very close.

Thank You for Your Son and in His name, I pray.

Amen.

_____
_____
_____
_____
_____
_____
_____
_____

The Sanctity of Singleness

Ephesians 3:20—21

[20] Now to him who is able to do immeasurably more than all we ask or imagine, according to his power that is at work within us, [21] to him be glory in the church and in Christ Jesus throughout all generations, for ever and ever! Amen.

Father God,

This scripture causes me to kneel before Your throne of grace with a humility that overwhelms my soul.

I cannot explain it because it is true. You continue to amaze me with what You do. You bless me with jobs that I don't deserve. You bless me with money I am subject to squander. You bless me with gifts that I don't use, and maybe not for Your glory when I do use them. You bless me and I complain. I do not use Your power that is at work within me consistently nor appropriately.

Lord, continue to help me. I want to give You all the honor, glory, and praise that I owe You, especially for the times that I was lazy and stingy.

In the name of Jesus, I pray.

Amen.

_____
_____
_____
_____
_____
_____
_____
_____

John 14:16—17

¹⁶ And I will ask the Father, and he will give you another advocate to help you and be with you forever— ¹⁷ the Spirit of truth. The world cannot accept him, because it neither sees him nor knows him. But you know him, for he lives with you and will be in you.

God,

Only You could give us Jesus. Then You add to Jesus the Holy Spirit!

Our Advocate because I need someone to plead my cases when I sin and am disobedient, and I cannot get my sorry self together to come to You as I should. Sometimes, I cannot own my sins, issues, and troubles.

Thank You for the gift of the Holy Spirit who helps me, according to Your will. The Holy Spirit shares with me what I should think about, pray about, and what I will see in the near future or eventually.

Lord, You have given me the understanding to hear and to be sensitive to the Holy Spirit. I value the Holy Spirit!

Thank You for an Advocate!

In the mighty name of Jesus, I pray.

Amen.

_____

_____

_____

_____

_____

_____

_____

The Sanctity of Singleness

John 16:12—15

¹² "I have much more to say to you, more than you can now bear. ¹³ But when he, the Spirit of truth, comes, he will guide you into all the truth. He will not speak on his own; he will speak only what he hears, and he will tell you what is yet to come. ¹⁴ He will glorify me because it is from me that he will receive what he will make known to you. ¹⁵ All that belongs to the Father is mine. That is why I said the Spirit will receive from me what he will make known to you."

God,

I wish I could be the type of child that Jesus is. I cannot seem to follow directions. I will wait on my directions from Jesus and the Holy Spirit.

I am trying to be sensitive to hear and to know the voice of the Holy Spirit. I eagerly await.

Thank You Father for the obedience of Jesus and the Holy Spirit. They both make life better.

In the powerful name of Jesus, I pray.

Amen.

_____
_____
_____
_____
_____
_____
_____

Matthew 6:5—8

⁵ "And when you pray, do not be like the hypocrites, for they love to pray standing in the synagogues and on the street corners to be seen by others. Truly I tell you, they have received their reward in full. ⁶ But when you pray, go into your room, close the door and pray to your Father, who is unseen. Then your Father, who sees what is done in secret, will reward you. ⁷ And when you pray, do not keep on babbling like pagans, for they think they will be heard because of their many words. ⁸ Do not be like them, for your Father knows what you need before you ask him.

Christ Jesus,

You teach me how to pray! I don't always pray like I should, but I want to pray more and in a way that pleases You.

Jesus, You do so much for me and I can't thank You enough. The least I could do would be to pray.

I do have a list of people I could pray for. I could pray for myself. I could pray for those that I go to church with, work with, friends with, and travel with. I can pray for people I don't know but I know that their situation exists: the unemployed, the homeless, the hurt, the depressed, the suppressed, and anyone else who is in pain, broken, bruised, and not quite whole. You taught me that too.

In the powerful name of Jesus, I pray.

Amen.

_____
_____
_____
_____
_____
_____

THE SANCTITY OF SINGLENESS

Matthew 6:9—13

⁹ "This, then, is how you should pray: "'Our Father in heaven, hallowed be your name,
¹⁰ your kingdom come, your will be done, on earth as it is in heaven.
¹¹ Give us today our daily bread.
¹² And forgive us our debts, as we also have forgiven our debtors.
¹³ And lead us not into temptation, but deliver us from the evil one.'

Jesus,

Thank You for the lesson.

Our Father in Heaven.

Holy is Thy name.

Your kingdom come.

Your will be done.

On Earth as it is in Heaven.

Give us this day our daily bread.

And forgive us those things we owe to others.

And help us to stay away from temptation.

And keep out of the clutches of the evil one.

Well Jesus that was sufficient for my needs and I thank You for the gift and power and sufficiency for prayer.

In the powerful name of Jesus, I pray.

Amen.

_____

_____

_____

Matthew 6:14—15; John 20:23

¹⁴ For if you forgive other people when they sin against you, your heavenly Father will also forgive you. ¹⁵ But if you do not forgive others their sins, your Father will not forgive your sins.

²³ If you forgive anyone's sins, their sins are forgiven; if you do not forgive them, they are not forgiven."

Father,

I want to be forgiven, especially by You. I have a hard time forgiving. I know that not forgiving others is against Your will.

Help me to forgive. Help me to forgive myself. Help me to be willing forgive willingly. Immediately. Unconditionally. Freely.

Thank You for reminding me to forgive. Lord, I need to be forgiven for being unforgiving. Lord, please forgive me as I forgive.

I will continue to forgive where I have. I will forgive where I have neglected to forgive.

In the wonderful name of Jesus, I pray.

Amen.

_____
_____
_____
_____
_____
_____
_____
_____

THE SANCTITY OF SINGLENESS

Matthew 6:16—18

[16] "When you fast, do not look somber as the hypocrites do, for they disfigure their faces to show others they are fasting. Truly I tell you, they have received their reward in full. [17] But when you fast, put oil on your head and wash your face, [18] so that it will not be obvious to others that you are fasting, but only to your Father, who is unseen; and your Father, who sees what is done in secret, will reward you.

Father God,

It is time to fast! So many issues and obstacles which cloud my judgement, all of which separate me from You.

Help me to fast. Help me to be disciplined when I fast.

Help me to pray properly when I fast. Show me Your will when I fast.

Lord, I remember the last time I fasted, I came out more focused. I was more intentional about praying and serving You.

Help me Father God to keep that focus after I fast.

Help me to fast regularly.

In the precious name of Jesus, I pray.

Amen.

_____
_____
_____
_____
_____
_____
_____

Matthew 6:22—23

²² "The eye is the lamp of the body. If your eyes are healthy, your whole body will be full of light. ²³ But if your eyes are unhealthy, your whole body will be full of darkness. If then the light within you is darkness, how great is that darkness!

Lord,

Let there be light within me! Lord! Let there be light in me! Lord, drive out the darkness in my life and my body! In the name of Jesus right now. I do not want darkness to be part of me. I do not want to live where darkness exists. I want to be light for You, God.

I want to shine in the dark places and drive away that darkness.

Keep me pure and upright before others so that I can please You, Lord, so that I can represent You, Father God.

Lord, remove darkness from my paths and those around me who inhabit darkness.

Cleanse my eyes and my heart and my total life so that I can see what You have for me to see.

In the complete name of Jesus, I pray.

Amen.

The Sanctity of Singleness

Matthew 6:24

²⁴ "No one can serve two masters. Either you will hate the one and love the other, or you will be devoted to the one and despise the other. You cannot serve both God and money.

Lord,

I want to serve You and only You! I cannot get this straight sometimes. I cannot help myself. I get excited about 'stuff' and get carried away and caught up.

Please help me to remain focused at all times.

I know that money and anything else is not going to help me or keep my soul safe from hurt or harm.

Lord, help me discern when this becomes a problem before it does so.

Help me to be an example to others as they walk closer to You.

In the matchless name of Jesus, I pray.

Amen.

_____
_____
_____
_____
_____
_____
_____
_____
_____

Matthew 6:25—34

[25] "Therefore I tell you, do not worry about your life, what you will eat or drink; or about your body, what you will wear. Is not life more than food, and the body more than clothes? [34] Therefore do not worry about tomorrow, for tomorrow will worry about itself. Each day has enough trouble of its own.

Father God,

I worry all of the time! I am so sorry that I do not know how not to worry. Oh Lord, I am so guilty about this worry and anxiety which stirs up within me. I am so consumed with what is next in my life, I cannot enjoy what is already happening in this life, especially You.

Help me to overcome my propensity to worry. You continue to remind me that You are the provider of my everything. I would have nothing without You. Everything I have belongs to You.

I should know that everything is in Your control. Every time, I think about what I worried about then how those things worked out, I know that I wasted valuable time, which I could have used to do something more valuable.

In the perfect name of Jesus, I pray.

Amen.

THE SANCTITY OF SINGLENESS

John 16:23—26

²³ In that day you will no longer ask me anything. Very truly I tell you, my Father will give you whatever you ask in my name. ²⁴ Until now you have not asked for anything in my name. Ask and you will receive, and your joy will be complete.

²⁵ "Though I have been speaking figuratively, a time is coming when I will no longer use this kind of language but will tell you plainly about my Father. ²⁶ In that day you will ask in my name. I am not saying that I will ask the Father on your behalf.

Lord,

I will ask in Your Son's name—for everything.

I do want things and achievements. I do want to be a leader and an expert in my field. I want to be respected, admired, and sought after.

But more importantly than all of that, I want to please You.

I do want what I ask for, but only if I can keep it and it does not interfere with our relationship.

Lord, thank You for the privilege of asking in the name of Jesus for what I desire.

In the outstanding name of Jesus, I pray.

Amen.

_____
_____
_____
_____
_____
_____
_____

John 16:33

³³ "I have told you these things, so that in me you may have peace. In this world you will have trouble. But take heart! I have overcome the world."

God,

Whew! Jesus has offered me His peace. Of all that He has to offer, His peace is of the most important and precious. In the order that it matters to me: His offered His life, then His love, and now His peace. Nothing else tops that.

Jesus reminds me that I will have trouble. The reminder does not help me to accept that trouble any easier. Jesus encourages me to take heart. Again, that trouble does not make me feel any better.

Jesus had overcome the world. The most important part is that He is telling me that I can get past this trouble. But that is because He and You are there to help me through.

In the excellent name of Jesus, I pray.

Amen.

_____
_____
_____
_____
_____
_____
_____
_____
_____
_____

The Sanctity of Singleness

John 17:1—5

After Jesus said this, he looked toward heaven and prayed:

"Father, the hour has come. Glorify your Son, that your Son may glorify you. [2] For you granted him authority over all people that he might give eternal life to all those you have given him. [3] Now this is eternal life: that they know you, the only true God, and Jesus Christ, whom you have sent. [4] I have brought you glory on earth by finishing the work you gave me to do. [5] And now, Father, glorify me in your presence with the glory I had with you before the world began.

Lord,

As Jesus prays, I am overwhelmed! I want to weep at the very visual of the time that this conversation takes place. Thank You, Jesus for Your sacrifice. Thank You for the lessons You have taught us during Your time on Earth.

Lord, my apologies for disappointing You. I fail the minor assignments, so I can understand why I do not earn the bigger assignments.

I pray to be better. Soon. So that I can give You the glory that You deserve. I do want to be able to complete the work that You have given me to do.

In the fabulous name of Jesus, I pray.

Amen.

_____
_____
_____
_____
_____
_____

John 17:6—19

[13] "I am coming to you now, but I say these things while I am still in the world, so that they may have the full measure of my joy within them. [14] I have given them your word and the world has hated them, for they are not of the world any more than I am of the world. [15] My prayer is not that you take them out of the world but that you protect them from the evil one. [16] They are not of the world, even as I am not of it. [17] Sanctify them by the truth; your word is truth. [18] As you sent me into the world, I have sent them into the world. [19] For them I sanctify myself, that they too may be truly sanctified.

Jesus,

When You pray for me, I blush. You prayed for my obedience. You honored God's selection of me, especially since I did not act like I was chosen. You prayed that I received Your wisdom, knowledge and understanding. You prayed that I understand love as You defined and for that I am grateful.

Christ, You prayed for my protection and You still do. I cannot thank You enough. Your prayers mean the world to me.

Lord, You declared me separate from the world and there I will stay.

You asked the Lord to sanctify me with His truth and that humbles me. I thank You for Your assignment in this world. I pray that I make You proud.

Thank You for praying for me.

In Your name, I pray.

Amen.

_____
_____
_____
_____

The Sanctity of Singleness

John 17:20—26

[24] "Father, I want those you have given me to be with me where I am, and to see my glory, the glory you have given me because you loved me before the creation of the world.

[25] "Righteous Father, though the world does not know you, I know you, and they know that you have sent me. [26] I have made you known to them, and will continue to make you known in order that the love you have for me may be in them and that I myself may be in them."

Jesus,

As You prayed for all believers, I was moved to pray as well.

Father, wherever believers are, so also are You. May we seek You daily—each minute of each day because You are our God and God alone.

May we continue to be receptive to You and heed Your word and Your will.

May You continue to forgive us and prayerfully we disappoint You a little bit less daily.

In the auspicious name of Jesus, I pray.

Amen.

Six Months of Solitude

John 14:10—11

[10] Don't you believe that I am in the Father, and that the Father is in me? The words I say to you I do not speak on my own authority. Rather, it is the Father, living in me, who is doing his work. [11] Believe me when I say that I am in the Father and the Father is in me; or at least believe on the evidence of the works themselves.

Lord,

You should not have to defend or prove Yourself to us at all! Jesus, You came to Earth to teach, to preach, to share God with us, and to save our sorry souls and no explanation is necessary. Thank You for coming and being obedient to God for us. None of us could have done what You have done for us.

Lord, I praise You for being Jesus and all that You do for me.

Lord, I thank You for the evidence which You have provided to me to let one know how much You love and care for me.

In the strong name of Jesus, I pray.

Amen.

_____
_____
_____
_____
_____
_____
_____
_____

THE SANCTITY OF SINGLENESS

John 13:34—35

[34] "A new command I give you: Love one another. As I have loved you, so you must love one another. [35] By this everyone will know that you are my disciples, if you love one another."

Lord,

Please help me to love people that I do not know. I want to love people like You do—with all of their faults and stuff. Right now, Lord, I only love a limited number of people based on some conditions and stipulations I have—none of which mirror what You use as the rule on how to love someone. Then Lord, I and Your help with unconditional, no matter what love.

I love people based on what they can do for me or what I want from them. Or how they look or how they make me feel. So I can stop 'loving' them when any of this changes.

I am grateful that You don't love like I do, but I need Your help.

In the profound name of Jesus, I pray.

Amen.

_____
_____
_____
_____
_____
_____
_____
_____

John 14:1—4

"Do not let your hearts be troubled. You believe in God; believe also in me. ² My Father's house has many rooms; if that were not so, would I have told you that I am going there to prepare a place for you? ³ And if I go and prepare a place for you, I will come back and take you to be with me that you also may be where I am. ⁴ You know the way to the place where I am going."

Jesus,

I love You! I believe that You were born of a virgin birth. I believe that You walked the Earth for 33 years without a single sin. I was impressed with Your throwing over that table at church.

I am more impressed with Your obedience and Your amazing love.

I believe that You were beaten for my iniquity and was abused for my sins. I believe that You walked on water to teach me some profound lessons.

I believe that You love me, and like no one else ever can or will.

I believe that You carried an old, rugged cross up a hill, where You were wounded—just for me! They buried You. You rose. Then ascended to Heaven.

I believe.

In the comfortable name of Jesus, I pray.

Amen.

_____

_____

_____

_____

_____

The Sanctity of Singleness

John 13:37—38; John 16:15—18, 25—27

³⁷ Peter asked, "Lord, why can't I follow you now? I will lay down my life for you."

³⁸ Then Jesus answered, "Will you really lay down your life for me? Very truly I tell you, before the rooster crows, you will disown me three times!"

Jesus,

I hope You don't spend as much time disciplining Peter as You do disciplining me.

Lord, I'll follow You anywhere. I look forward to when we will in person. I know that we will have lots of things to talk about.

Thank You for Your provision for me. I am ever grateful. I am consumed with what You do for me. I am overwhelmed by Your presence and Your words. When I read about some of Your interactions, I am just captivated with some of what You say, such that I hope that You will say that to me and other words, I am definitely trying to avoid. But some which absolutely move me in a mighty way are: Come; Do you want to walk; and, Daughter, your faith has made you whole.

In the miraculous name of Jesus, I pray.

Amen.

_____

_____

_____

_____

_____

_____

John 12:1—8

⁴ But one of his disciples, Judas Iscariot, who was later to betray him, objected, ⁵ "Why wasn't this perfume sold and the money given to the poor? It was worth a year's wages." ⁶ He did not say this because he cared about the poor but because he was a thief; as keeper of the money bag, he used to help himself to what was put into it.

⁷ "Leave her alone," Jesus replied. "It was intended that she should save this perfume for the day of my burial. ⁸ You will always have the poor among you, but you will not always have me."

Lord,

May I have wisdom like Mary's so that I can know when to stop, to serve and to worship You!

Mary did not hesitate to worship, nor did she consider what would be said when she did!

Lord, sometimes I act just like Martha and Judas—worried about the wrong thing; concluded with the wrong details rather than You—the main focus of the scene and situation.

Finally, Lord help me to stay focused on You and not the noise which exists around me. Father, I thank You for making it plan, AGAIN, how I should behave and respond to Your presence.

In the immaculate of Jesus, I pray.

Amen.

_____
_____
_____
_____
_____

THE SANCTITY OF SINGLENESS

John 13:10—11

¹⁰ Jesus answered, "Those who have had a bath need only to wash their feet; their whole body is clean. And you are clean, though not every one of you." ¹¹ For he knew who was going to betray him, and that was why he said not everyone was clean.

Father,

Oh how I want to be clean! I don't want to embarrass You as I often do. I want to be clean and whole, seen as complete in Your eyes.

I may not be Judas and would never do exactly what he did, but my sins are still sins. Lord, please help me to stop sinning in the same way as I always have. I should be more mature than to keep repeating the same sin regularly.

Lord, even when I sin, You let me experience some dignity, although I deserve immediate death. I thank You for Your love and Your steadfast guidance over my life. I love You and thank You for washing my feet.

In the unparalleled name of Jesus, I pray.

Amen.

_____
_____
_____
_____
_____
_____
_____

John 3:16

[16] For God so loved the world that he gave his one and only Son, that whoever believes in him shall not perish but have eternal life.

God,

For You loved me, so that You gave up Your One and Only Son so that I may live! Oh Lord, I ask myself all of the time if I would or could give up my children for the rest of an ungrateful, disobedient, sinful and faithless people, such as myself.

Thank You for Your Son and the gift that He is to me.

I know that I cannot repay You for Your Son and Your sacrifice, but I want to show You my gratitude.

Father, thank You for demonstrating Your excellence so that I have an example. I still weep when I hear and recite this verse.

In the prophetic name of Jesus, I pray.

Amen.

_____
_____
_____
_____
_____
_____
_____
_____
_____

The Sanctity of Singleness

John 15:12—17

¹² My command is this: Love each other as I have loved you. ¹³ Greater love has no one than this: to lay down one's life for one's friends.

Father God,

Jesus gave a command that You have given several times before: LOVE. Lord, You want me to love You, myself, and everybody else. Lord, I know that I don't love You like I should. I am not obedient like I should be.

Lord, one of the reasons that I cannot love others is because I don't love myself that much. I have problems accepting myself at time at face value, and definitely not like how You see me. Lord, help me to love myself like You do. I want to love others because You said to.

The others reason is that some people don't deserve my love. But that means that I don't deserve the love of others either.

In the loving name of Jesus, I pray.

Amen.

_____
_____
_____
_____
_____
_____
_____
_____

John 20:22

²² And with that he breathed on them and said, "Receive the Holy Spirit. ²³ If you forgive anyone's sins, their sins are forgiven; if you do not forgive them, they are not forgiven."

God,

When Jesus gifts us with Your powerful and perfect peace. It is such a settling presence. It calms my fears and sets aside my doubts—when I allow His peace to overtake me.

But when You give me the Holy Spirit. Letting me receive the Holy Spirit into my sinful being is a gift.

But then Jesus, You breathed on me! You breathed like on me at birth. You breathed on my body to heal me and to love me. Now, You breathed on me to share the Holy Spirit.

Thank You for that Father! I need all that You have breathed on me.

Because You told me I could ask in Your name, I pray.

Amen.

The Sanctity of Singleness

John 20:24—29

²⁶ A week later his disciples were in the house again, and Thomas was with them. Though the doors were locked, Jesus came and stood among them and said, "Peace be with you!" ²⁷ Then he said to Thomas, "Put your finger here; see my hands. Reach out your hand and put it into my side. Stop doubting and believe."

²⁸ Thomas said to him, "My Lord and my God!"

²⁹ Then Jesus told him, "Because you have seen me, you have believed; blessed are those who have not seen and yet have believed."

God,

Thank You for being patient with me like You were with Thomas. You explained to him something You did not have to explain.

You don't owe me anything, but You shared it all anyway.

I am not supposed to beg You to do anything. You don't have to prove Your presence and Your aliveness to me.

I have enough evidence. Help me to recognize Your evidence so that I don't have to keep asking You these same simple questions. Help me to trust!

I pray in Your name because You said I should.

Amen.

Luke 22:7—23

[17] After taking the cup, he gave thanks and said, "Take this and divide it among you. [18] For I tell you I will not drink again from the fruit of the vine until the kingdom of God comes."

[19] And he took bread, gave thanks and broke it, and gave it to them, saying, "This is my body given for you; do this in remembrance of me."

[20] In the same way, after the supper he took the cup, saying, "This cup is the new covenant in my blood, which is poured out for you. [21] But the hand of him who is going to betray me is with mine on the table. [22] The Son of Man will go as it has been decreed. But woe to that man who betrays him!" [23] They began to question among themselves which of them it might be who would do this.

Father God,

Thank You for the Holy Communion. You served us with Your blood and Your body. The wine that You served represents the blood that You would shed for my life as the redemption of my sins and for my foolishness and bad choices.

The unleavened bread which represents Your body which was bruised for the future sins that I would commit.

Lord, I am so humbled. When You serve us, I am so overwhelmed when You serve us and gift us.

In the auspicious name of Jesus, I pray.

Amen.

The Sanctity of Singleness

Luke 22:31—32

³¹ "Simon, Simon, Satan has asked to sift all of you as wheat. ³² But I have prayed for you, Simon, that your faith may not fail. And when you have turned back, strengthen your brothers."

Lord,

I wish and pray that You would say no to the devil when he asks to sift me or to tempt, or test me. I am not Job, or Peter, or David, and I appreciate the trust and confidence You have in me. I recognize that Your faith in me is stronger than my faith in myself. I just want to please You and not disappoint You, but I wish I could not that without the presence of Satan.

Help me to meet Your expectations. Thank You for praying me when I have been asked for by satan.

Father God, keep watch over my faith and my walk during these seasons.

I want to be favored like David, Ruth, Naomi, Joseph, Peter and Job, but that means I have to endure what they have as well.

In the excellent name of Jesus, I pray.

Amen.

_____
_____
_____
_____
_____
_____
_____

All About the Mate

THE SANCTITY OF SINGLENESS

Ephesians 5:22—23

²² Wives, submit yourselves to your own husbands as you do to the Lord. ²³ For the husband is the head of the wife as Christ is the head of the church, his body, of which he is the Savior.

Lord,

So if I get married, there's submission to consider?! Lord, I need to pray over my ability to submit and my potential mate's potential to submit as well.

Lord, submission is important but it is hard. Help us both to submit to You and to each other according to Your will and directions.

Lord, help us to avoid listening to the nay-sayers who will speak against the beauty of submission.

Until You reveal and give me to my mate and vice versa, I will submit to You, God.

In the fabulous name of Jesus, I pray.

Amen.

_____
_____
_____
_____
_____
_____
_____
_____

Ephesians 5:24

²⁴ Now as the church submits to Christ, so also wives should submit to their husbands in everything.

Lord,

Help me and my mate to submit to You and to one another as You have written in Your word.

Lord, help us to submit to Your will and Your way. Lord, help us avoid all selfish ambition and personal agendas.

Help us keep You first in our lives in such a way that others see You through us. Father, help us live so that others ask how and why and we give You all the glory and honor.

Lord, we love You individually and we will love You collectively.

Because You told me to ask in Your name, I pray.

Amen.

_____
_____
_____
_____
_____
_____
_____
_____

THE SANCTITY OF SINGLENESS

Ephesians 5:25—27

²⁵ Husbands, love your wives, just as Christ loved the church and gave himself up for her ²⁶ to make her holy, cleansing[a] her by the washing with water through the word, ²⁷ and to present her to himself as a radiant church, without stain or wrinkle or any other blemish, but holy and blameless.

Father God,

May I hear these words for the nourishment and health of my relationships. May I be the neighbor who is able to speak truth to the other. Lord, may I keep my anger under control so that I do not sin. I do not know my capabilities and do not want to know.

I want to please You and serve You. I want to seek You and hear from You. I do not want my sin to stop me from hearing from You or being heard.

Lord, help me to remember that Your wrath is more powerful, more purposed, more important, and more ordered than my wrath will ever be. My wrath does not contradict Yours, nor does it over take Yours.

In the precious name of Jesus, I pray.

Amen.

_____
_____
_____
_____
_____
_____
_____
_____
_____

Ephesians 5:28

²⁸ In this same way, husbands ought to love their wives as their own bodies. He who loves his wife loves himself.

Lord,

Are You saying that I will only love another as much as I love myself? Oh Lord, bless Your holy name! That's a revelation! Lord, help me love myself enough to love others especially my mate the way You designed for me to love.

Lord, I cannot believe that all this time that my self—love and the lack thereof was impacting what I thought I could afford to give others.

I want to love others like I am supposed to love myself, but I fall short regularly, like all of the time.

Lord, help me with love of You, myself, and others.

In the extraordinary name of Jesus, I pray.

Amen.

The Sanctity of Singleness

Ephesians 5:29—30

²⁹ After all, no one ever hated their own body, but they feed and care for their body, just as Christ does the church— ³⁰ for we are members of his body.

Lord,

As low as my self-esteem has been at times, it is hard to tell if I hate myself or not. I know that I should not but sometimes I do.

It is hard to love others when I hate me. I need help to stop hating myself. I need help to appreciate Your work and the fact that You love me.

I am trying to find reasons to stop hating my own body.

Lord, I need help using Your lens to see myself.

In the auspicious name of Jesus, I pray.

Amen.

Ephesians 5:31

³¹ "For this reason a man will leave his father and mother and be united to his wife, and the two will become one flesh."

Father God,

I have heard and read that this meddling of family will disrupt and even end marriages. Help me to remember that I am to leave and cleave.

Help me to understand how to separate the two entities: my mate and my family. Help me to not compare the mate to the parents. Help me to only do what does not cause my family and friends to feel angry and terrible toward my mate.

Lord, help me to stay focused on a God—centered relationship, minimizing the unnecessary issues, not letting the past effect today, and loving without conditions.

I pray this prayer in the loving name of Jesus.

Amen.

The Sanctity of Singleness

Ephesians 5:32—33

[32] This is a profound mystery—but I am talking about Christ and the church. [33] However, each one of you also must love his wife as he loves himself, and the wife must respect her husband.

Father God,

I pray to understand more of the mysteries of You and Christ. I know I may never but I will commit to try to understand. I submit to understand more of what You want my focus on and much less of me.

I am still blessed and overwhelmed by the relationship with the Church and us!

Lord, I want to love my mate and respect my mate as You have prescribed. Love is hard to give and manage. Respect is even harder.

Lord, help me to love others like You love me—unconditional and completely. Help me offer respect, especially when I feel that it is undeserved and I don't feel like it.

It is in the incredible name of Jesus, I pray.

Amen.

Ephesians 4:32

³² Be kind and compassionate to one another, forgiving each other, just as in Christ God forgave you.

Lord,

Help me to be kind and compassionate to others, especially when I do not want to or do not see a need to be. Lord, help me when I do not feel others deserve my kindness and compassion.

Let me offer kindness and compassion even when I do not know the reason for it.

Lord, help me to forgive others because Jesus died so that I can be forgiven. Help me to willingly forgive. So much so that others are in awe, as am I, of what You are doing through me.

Thank You for forgiving me of my awful sins. Thank You for keeping me cleansed and whole.

In the blessed name of Jesus, I pray.

Amen.

The Sanctity of Singleness

1 Peter 4:8

⁸ Above all, love each other deeply, because love covers over a multitude of sins.

Lord,

You have told us many times that love is powerful. You have demonstrated many times that love has exclusive powers.

Lord, I have overlooked the power of love. And the influence of love. And the widespread contagion of love.

Lord, I have rejected the love of You and others in my life such I may grow through that love. Forgive me for rejecting Your love and those whom You have sent to love me and those You sent me to love.

Lord, help me to love freely! Unconditionally! Lord, help me to see everybody who I am supposed to love. Help me to love myself! Love covers over a multitude of sins! That verse overwhelms me!

In the dynamic name of Jesus, I pray.

Amen.

Proverbs 19:22

²² What a person desires is unfailing love;
  better to be poor than a liar.

Lord,

I know that my love will NEVER match Yours, but let me <u>not</u> fail anyone that I love or that You have given me to love! I want unfailing love too! I want to be the object of someone's unconditional love. I want to be a loving representative of You! At all times!

Lord, help me to offer unfailing and unconditional love so that I will please You and represent You. The other recipient of my love is also Your vessel. I do not want to mistreat them.

Love is powerful—You taught us that through the demonstration of Your Son's birth!

In the impactful name of Jesus, I pray.

Amen.

The Sanctity of Singleness

1 Corinthians 7:3

³ The husband should fulfill his marital duty to his wife, and likewise the wife to her husband.

Lord,

May I be attentive to my mate as defined by Your word. Lord, I have heard about mates neglecting each other and I know that some of that has led to the demise of their marriage. I don't want to be that statistic of divorce or separation. I don't want to wait this long time only to have discord in my marriage.

Lord, prepare my heart and mind to serve my mate, according to Your will.

Lord, let me not be selfish with my fulfillment of my martial duty. Also, let me be compassionate toward my mate when the marital duty is not fulfilled.

Lord, let me be forgiving and forgiven in this matter.

In the special name of Jesus, I pray.

Amen.

_____
_____
_____
_____
_____
_____
_____
_____

1 Corinthians 7:4

⁴ The wife does not have authority over her own body but yields it to her husband. In the same way, the husband does not have authority over his own body but yields it to his wife.

Father God,

I hear that this is a strong issue and is tearing apart many marriages. I do now want to get married to get divorced. I don't want to cause displeasure to my mate. I want to offer myself to my mate at all of the appropriate times.

Lord, help me to refrain from withholding my body from my mate unless we are fasting and have agreed to not to be intimate.

Help me Lord not to withhold my body to hurt my mate or to use my body as a bargaining chip.

Lord, help me to meet my mate's needs and do not let the devil get a foothold.

In the sovereign name of Jesus, I pray.

Amen.

_____
_____
_____
_____
_____
_____
_____
_____
_____

The Sanctity of Singleness

1 Corinthians 7:5

⁵ Do not deprive each other except perhaps by mutual consent and for a time, so that you may devote yourselves to prayer. Then come together again so that Satan will not tempt you because of your lack of self-control.

Lord,

Please help me not to deprive my mate out of anger or selfishness, bitterness or malice, privilege or vengeance. Lord, make me inclined to my mate such that I always want to engage with my mate on that level. Lord, allow us the wisdom to know when to fast from intimacy and when to return to each other.

Lord, help us to pray together as we fast. We are fasting to hear from You, to get closer to You, and to crave each other more according to Your will.

Father, I plead with You to keep satan away from our union.

It is in the fabulous name of Jesus, I pray.

Amen.

_____
_____
_____
_____
_____
_____
_____

Six Months of Solitude

1 Corinthians 7:6—7

⁶ I say this as a concession, not as a command. ⁷ I wish that all of you were as I am. But each of you has your own gift from God; one has this gift, another has that.

Lord,

Help me see what my mate needs and what my mate wants; help me to be sensitive to my mate. Let us compatible and amenable to each other in all of our marriage and relationship.

Lord, keep our hearts intertwined and committed to one another, loving one another.

Lord, keep us close to You so that we can grow closer to each other.

Lord, help us to be gracious to each other.

Help us to be considerate and compassionate to each other.

Lord, help us to keep the peace which Jesus provides.

In the keeping name of Jesus, I pray.

Amen.

_____

_____

_____

_____

_____

_____

_____

_____

The Sanctity of Singleness

1 Corinthians 7:10—11

[10] To the married I give this command (not I, but the Lord): A wife must not separate from her husband. [11] But if she does, she must remain unmarried or else be reconciled to her husband. And a husband must not divorce his wife.

Lord,

I pray not to be a statistic! I pray to be a mate that does not influence divorce. I pray to be someone that another person does not want to divorce or quarrel.

Lord, help us to be amenable and loving, consistent in our communication, not failing each other.

Lord, help us to seek You in the difficult times and stay committed to You when times are great.

Lord, help us to keep an humble spirit in all that we do and are to each other.

May You bless our marriage to not to be a statistic and something that does not please You or bring You glory.

In the forgiving name of Jesus, I pray.

Amen.

_____
_____
_____
_____
_____
_____
_____

1 Corinthians 7:12—15a

[12] To the rest I say this (I, not the Lord): If any brother has a wife who is not a believer and she is willing to live with him, he must not divorce her. [13] And if a woman has a husband who is not a believer and he is willing to live with her, she must not divorce him. [14] For the unbelieving husband has been sanctified through his wife, and the unbelieving wife has been sanctified through her believing husband. Otherwise your children would be unclean, but as it is, they are holy. [15] But if the unbeliever leaves, let it be so.

Lord,

I pray to not be married to an unbeliever. It seems so much harder than to be married to someone who already loves You.

Lord, I want to please You. I don't want to upset or disappoint You.

I don't want to seem closed to the idea, but it just seems unreasonable to fall in love with someone who does not love You.

I pray that I am sensitive to Your urgings and open to Your will.

In the fantastic name of Jesus, I pray.

Amen.

_____
_____
_____
_____
_____
_____
_____
_____

The Sanctity of Singleness

1 Corinthians 7:15b

The brother or the sister is not bound in such circumstances; God has called us to live in peace.

Lord,

May You provide me Your peace! I am in need of Your peace. Your peace transcends my total understanding.

Lord, help me to be peaceful. I want to find peace in chaos. I want to dismiss chaos and confusion with Your peace. Father, I want to embody Your peace in such a way that others are forced to be peaceful in my presence.

Lord, I want to share Your peace with my mate and my family, friends and community.

May I share peace everywhere I go. Let me be peaceful in my soul.

In the auspicious name of Jesus, I pray.

Amen.

_____

_____

_____

_____

_____

_____

_____

_____

_____

Matthew 19:6

⁶ So they are no longer two, but one flesh. Therefore what God has joined together, let no one separate."

Sovereign Father,

May I understand as a partner how important these words are to my future mate, and our relationship.

May I be able to express my commitment through the intentional commitment to my mate.

Lord, help me become one my mate that You have chosen for me. Because You have joined us, please let us not get in Your way or try to separate what You have joined. Lord, let me be mindful at all times that this is Your will.

Father, help me keep focused on Your will.

In the wise name of Jesus, I pray.

Amen.

_____
_____
_____
_____
_____
_____
_____
_____
_____
_____

The Sanctity of Singleness

Hebrews 13:4

⁴ Marriage should be honored by all, and the marriage bed kept pure, for God will judge the adulterer and all the sexually immoral.

God,

May You bless the future union. Help me be the mate You designed. Help me to be an honorable spouse. Help me to keep our bed undefiled. Help keep me away from temptation. Let me remain focused on what You have in mind.

Marriage is special the way You created it. Help me keep the specialness of the union daily. Help me to not be quarrelsome or cantankerous, disrespectful, or insensitive. Help me the type of mate that protects my mate that protects my mate from harm, especially any hurt or harm that I personally inflict.

Let me be forgiving, loving, respectful, and compassionate.

In the awesome name of Jesus, I pray.

Amen.

_____
_____
_____
_____
_____
_____
_____
_____
_____

2 Samuel 12:24—25

[24] Then David comforted his wife Bathsheba, and he went to her and made love to her. She gave birth to a son, and they named him Solomon. The LORD loved him; [25] and because the LORD loved him, he sent word through Nathan the prophet to name him Jedidiah.
Father,

I am overwhelmed by the depth of the story of Bathsheba and David. Lord, I want to make love to my spouse like David made love to Bathsheba. I want to be made love to by my spouse like David made love to Bathsheba.

I want to have a union which pleases You the way Bathsheba and David gained Your favor.

Father, I respect their sensitivity to each other during good times and bad. They came together after a tragedy, but some couples never survive this type of crisis. Help us survive and thrive through all events.

In the consoling name of Jesus, I pray.

Amen.

_____
_____
_____
_____
_____
_____
_____
_____
_____
_____

THE SANCTITY OF SINGLENESS

Genesis 2:24—25, 4:1—2

[24] That is why a man leaves his father and mother and is united to his wife, and they become one flesh.
[25] Adam and his wife were both naked, and they felt no shame.
Adam made love to his wife Eve, and she became pregnant and gave birth to Cain. She said, "With the help of the LORD I have brought forth a man." [2] Later she gave birth to his brother Abel. Now Abel kept flocks, and Cain worked the soil.

Father God,

May I be dedicated to my mate the way You designed. Lord, I know that Eve and Adam were not great examples in some areas, but in this instance, they are great examples and I thank You for that example.

Lord, I want to be dedicated, committed, loved, loving, and focused on my mate. And I pray that my mate feels and treats me the same way.

God, help us see each other the way You see us individually and as one. Keep us grounded, faithful, committed, and connected.

I pray for the solid emotional connection with my mate. Thank You God for that connection.

In the victorious name of Jesus, I pray.

Amen.

Genesis 7:1—5, 13

7 The LORD then said to Noah, "Go into the ark, you and your whole family, because I have found you righteous in this generation. ² Take with you seven pairs of every kind of clean animal, a male and its mate, and one pair of every kind of unclean animal, a male and its mate, ³ and also seven pairs of every kind of bird, male and female, to keep their various kinds alive throughout the earth. ⁴ Seven days from now I will send rain on the earth for forty days and forty nights, and I will wipe from the face of the earth every living creature I have made."
⁵ And Noah did all that the LORD commanded him.

Lord,

Oh Lord! May I be patient to see, understand, hear, follow, and obey the will of God!

Lord, I am thankful for the example of Noah and his wife. She did not argue. She did not negate or interfere with Noah's work. She seemed really cooperative.

Noah probably questioned You, God. But he was still obedient to You. Thank You for giving us an example like Noah. He did a great work with a wife, who had to do a great amount of participation, not voluntarily. Thank You for their example of marriage and marital cooperativeness that they exhibited. Lord, may I be blessed with the cooperative nature and spirit which keeps our marriage whole.

In the passionate name of Jesus, I pray.

Amen.

THE SANCTITY OF SINGLENESS

Genesis 21:1—7

21 Now the LORD was gracious to Sarah as he had said, and the LORD did for Sarah what he had promised. **²** Sarah became pregnant and bore a son to Abraham in his old age, at the very time God had promised him. **³** Abraham gave the name Isaac[a] to the son Sarah bore him. **⁴** When his son Isaac was eight days old, Abraham circumcised him, as God commanded him. **⁵** Abraham was a hundred years old when his son Isaac was born to him.
⁶ Sarah said, "God has brought me laughter, and everyone who hears about this will laugh with me." **⁷** And she added, "Who would have said to Abraham that Sarah would nurse children? Yet I have borne him a son in his old age."

Sovereign God,

It took one hundred years for Abraham to have a child with Sarah. She was 90 years old! Patience had gone awry. But You still gave them a baby! You could have said no. You could have changed Your mind.

Mighty God, thank You for grace as we try to live according to Your will and sometimes we don't try and You still offer us Your undeserved grace.

Help me to not be like Sarah and Abraham—anxious and controlling. Help me to wait on You and Your will so that I can live according to Your will and purpose.

Father, continue to bless me as only You can.

In the patient name of Jesus, I pray.

Amen.

_____
_____
_____
_____
_____

Six Months of Solitude

Ruth 4:13—15, 21—22

¹³ So Boaz took Ruth and she became his wife. When he made love to her, the LORD enabled her to conceive, and she gave birth to a son. ¹⁴ The women said to Naomi: "Praise be to the LORD, who this day has not left you without a guardian-redeemer. May he become famous throughout Israel! ¹⁵ He will renew your life and sustain you in your old age. For your daughter-in-law, who loves you and who is better to you than seven sons, has given him birth."

Lord,

If we could research our family legacy in this manner, then we could make better decisions. If You allow me, then I will lead a legacy just like Ruth, the great-grandmother of King David and the lineage of Jesus. I pray to be a leader as a parent and a mate, such that our family will live according to Your will and bring You deserved glory.

I can start with one such that I am concerned with Your commands and decrees.

Ruth and Boaz had to consider tribal rules and while some of that no longer exists, I can follow the rule of a legacy and protecting the family name.

In the illustrious name of Jesus, I pray.

Amen.

_____
_____
_____
_____
_____
_____

The Sanctity of Singleness

1 Samuel 1: 5, 8

⁵ But to Hannah he gave a double portion because he loved her, and the LORD had closed her womb. ⁸ Her husband Elkanah would say to her, "Hannah, why are you weeping? Why don't you eat? Why are you downhearted? Don't I mean more to you than ten sons?"

Lord,

I never want to be so consumed with something that either You or my mate feels like that something is more important than either of You.

Lord, thank You for Hannah and Elkanah's story of transparency and love. It is what I aspire to be with my mate.

I don't want to feel like Elkanah feels and I definitely don't want to make someone feel like Elkanah felt when he asked her wasn't he more important than 10 sons.

Lord, remind me to affirm my mate, listen to my mate, love my mate, forgive my mate, and have compassion for my mate.

In the peaceful name of Jesus, I pray.

Amen.

_____
_____
_____
_____
_____
_____
_____
_____

Esther 5:3

³ Then the king asked, "What is it, Queen Esther? What is your request? Even up to half the kingdom, it will be given you."

Lord,

May I be reminded of the favor that the King offered Esther. May our favor toward each other be mutual, consistent, loving, forgiving, and overwhelming.

May we consider each other's feelings about our own. All of the time; especially when we don't want to and when we don't like the topic or proposal. May we be concerned with the feelings of the other person before our own. May we not take advantage of the other person in any situation.

Lord, I pray that nor matter what happens that we find a way to love each other, to forgive each other, to encourage each other, and be honorable to each other.

In the awesome name of Jesus, I pray.

Amen.

The Sanctity of Singleness

Job 2:9—10

⁹ His wife said to him, "Are you still maintaining your integrity? Curse God and die!" ¹⁰ He replied, "You are talking like a foolish woman. Shall we accept good from God, and not trouble?" In all this, Job did not sin in what he said.

Lord,

May all that I do edify and bring glory to You. May I not be an argumentative or cantankerous mate, such that my mate may distance themselves from me.

Father God, I do not want to lead my mate astray. I do not want to be upset with You because of how my mate is treated or what they suffered because You don't trust them to be stifled by satan. Likewise, I don't want my mate to behave like Job's wife. Further, I don't want to believe like her either.

Lord, I know that You will permit us to be tested. I pray that I can behave like Job in a manner that pleases You completely.

Father, I love You. I will love my mate. I pray to never been in conflict with You because of my mate's view of our relationship.

In the magnificent name of Jesus, I pray.

Amen.

Six Months of Solitude

Matthew 1:18—25

[20] But after he had considered this, an angel of the Lord appeared to him in a dream and said, "Joseph son of David, do not be afraid to take Mary home as your wife, because what is conceived in her is from the Holy Spirit. [21] She will give birth to a son, and you are to give him the name Jesus, because he will save his people from their sins."

Master,

I am still overwhelmed by the entire story of Mary and Joseph. I ask myself what would I do if that had been me. If I were Joseph, then how would I have handled it? Would I have done what Joseph contemplated? He seemed so mature about the matter.

Lord, if only I could handle such a serious matter like Mary did. Do You trust me like You trusted Mary? What can I do to be trusted like Mary and Joseph?

Lord, forgive me for previously mishandling other serious matters with which You trusted me. I pray that I certainly do not mishandle the mate You send to me. I pray that You help manage what You trust and gift me with. I do not want to disappoint You. I do not want to misrepresent You either.

In the magnanimous of name of Jesus, I pray.

Amen.

_____

_____

_____

_____

_____

_____

The Sanctity of Singleness

Luke 1:5—25

²³ When his time of service was completed, he returned home. ²⁴ After this his wife Elizabeth became pregnant and for five months remained in seclusion. ²⁵ "The Lord has done this for me," she said. "In these days he has shown his favor and taken away my disgrace among the people."

God,

In the tradition of that time, I would estimate that they married when she was 15 years old, which means that they were married for 73 years. In their entire marriage, they were alone—no one to buffer or argue over. I cannot imagine how they reconciled and were reminded that they each are enough for each other. You have taught us that we do not need an additional person to be considered a whole person. Further, You have taught that we are whole as a couple and do not need a child to make us a family.

Lord, May I forever be able to keep that separate and understood.

In the bold name of Jesus, I pray.

Amen.

_____

_____

_____

_____

_____

_____

_____

Six Months of Solitude

1 Corinthians 13:13 (MSG)

¹³ But for right now, until that completeness, we have three things to do to lead us toward that consummation: Trust steadily in God, hope unswervingly, love extravagantly. And the best of the three is love.

God,

I want to. I really do, but the last time I loved at that level of extravagance, I left so broken and so hurt that I did not think I would survive.

You have demonstrated extravagant love by giving us You Son. You also have shown us by the couples You share in Your word and the world. I pray to be an example couple; an example mate.

Help me to love extravagantly, even to strangers and colleagues. Help me to give away the love that only You provide and replenish for me to give away.

Help me to receive the love like You designed from others, especially You.

In the courageous name of Jesus, I pray.

Amen.

THE SANCTITY OF SINGLENESS

Song of Solomon

God,

Help us keep our bedroom pure and exciting. Help us remain aroused by the other, interested and engaging, loving and fulfilling. Lord, help us to keep the world out of our business and affairs. Help us to keep our eyes trained only on each other.

Let us strive daily to find and to experience the fresh and new. Let us listen attentively and compassionately.

Keep us as one so that the enemy's attempts to separate us will be futile.

Father, we need Your hand as our glue to remain steadfast in pleasing one another. We want to be our best for each other. In every possible way.

In the precious name of Jesus, I pray.

Amen.

_____
_____
_____
_____
_____
_____
_____
_____
_____

Characteristics Of a Single Person

The Sanctity of Singleness

Ephesians 4:26—27

[26] "In your anger do not sin": Do not let the sun go down while you are still angry, [27] and do not give the devil a foothold.

Father,

You know me and everything about me, especially what makes me angry and the consequences after that. I do not want to disappoint You. Help my anger to be minimized and to have peace in You when it happens that I want to give the devil a foothold by sinning.

Lord, please help me assess situations differently based on the anger that I have previously expressed.

Thank You for Your control over me. Never allow my anger to negatively affect my mate. Or harm my mate. In any way.

Lord, help me to direct anger to help the good of others.

In the omnipotent name of Jesus, I pray.

Amen.

_____
_____
_____
_____
_____
_____
_____
_____
_____

Luke 6:32—33

³² "If you love those who love you, what credit is that to you? Even sinners love those who love them. ³³ And if you do good to those who are good to you, what credit is that to you? Even sinners do that.

Lord,

I am so embarrassed and ashamed that I am that verse. I do that. I am not representing You well at all. How can I be a vessel, a disciple, if I only love those I know? Why can't I take the risk? I should be able to but I can't. I don't. Father, help me to increase my ability to want to love others and open my heart as it should be so that I can love and hold others close as You command.

Father, help me to not be stingy so that I can love others. You send strangers to me regularly who are in need of love as I am. I want to remember that You are the filler and the provider of my love and I have never run out of love. I thank You for keeping me in Your loving arms even when I don't love others like I should.

In the loving name of Jesus, I pray.

Amen.

The Sanctity of Singleness

1 Corinthians 13

⁴ Love is patient, love is kind. It does not envy, it does not boast, it is not proud. ⁵ It does not dishonor others, it is not self-seeking, it is not easily angered, it keeps no record of wrongs. ⁶ Love does not delight in evil but rejoices with the truth. ⁷ It always protects, always trusts, always hopes, always perseveres.

Lord,

I pray to be those verses: every word in it. I want to love and to be love and to be loved. Your word says that love covers over a multitude of sins.

I want to love someone past their hurt. I pray to love someone past their hurt. I pray to love someone to their appropriate level of worth by Your definition. I want to be identified as a loving person, such that others week me for move and that they are assured of Your love through me.

I pray to love like You designed and have commanded. I know that I am defensive when others try. I also realize that I need to be more of the characteristics You teach. I need to espouse more of those traits so that I will be the Christian You need me to be.

In the powerful name of Jesus, I pray.

Amen.

_____
_____
_____
_____
_____
_____
_____

1 Corinthians 13:13 (MSG)

¹³ But for right now, until that completeness, we have three things to do to lead us toward that consummation: Trust steadily in God, hope unswervingly, love extravagantly. And the best of the three is love.

Father God,

For the example that You provide for love, I am grateful. The first time I read this verse in the version, I was overwhelmed because of what the word extravagant means.

Lord, I want to love extravagantly! I want to give others move love than they deserve. I really want to. I want to be transparent when I love and love authentically.

I need Your help reaching Your definition of extravagance. You did it when You created the world. You did it when You created me. You did it when You saved my soul. You did it when You promised me that Your Son would die for my sins. You did when it You kept Your word and gave us Jesus who was hung, He bled, and died for me because You love me extravagantly. I pray to do a fraction of that but much more than I do now.

In the mighty name of Jesus, I pray.

Amen.

_____
_____
_____
_____
_____
_____
_____
_____

THE SANCTITY OF SINGLENESS

Nehemiah 1:5—6

⁵ Then I said:
"LORD, the God of heaven, the great and awesome God, who keeps his covenant of love with those who love him and keep his commandments, ⁶ let your ear be attentive and your eyes open to hear the prayer your servant is praying before you day and night for your servants, the people of Israel. I confess the sins we Israelites, including myself and my father's family, have committed against you.

Father God,

When Nehemiah prayed and wept, mourned and fasted, he prayed about You and described You as the God who keeps His covenant of love. I learned that love is a covenant. That just changed my life! Lord, thank You for Your word that just ministered to my attitude about love.

Lord, heal me from my attitude about love because I believed that love can start and end. Covenant, which You created and defined is a formal, solemn agreement of conditional promises. This covenant of love is based on Your unconditional love for me and my love and obedience to You.

Lord, thank You for Your covenant of love, forgiving me of my sins, and help me to love according to a covenant, rather than a whim.

In the loving name of Jesus, I pray.

Amen.

_____
_____
_____
_____
_____
_____

Matthew 5:44

⁴⁴ But I tell you, love your enemies and pray for those who persecute you,

Lord,

I thought that You asked for some difficult behavior before, but now You are really asking for something difficult. You want me to love people that not only do not love me, they also mean to harm me. They have persecuted, accused me, slandered me, and have tried to keep me away from what could be mine. They try to keep me distracted from You with their antics.

Father, I have tried to keep my heart and mind and soul committed to You during these difficult times. I pray that You help me in this time when so many people are trying to harm me but I still need to love them.

Help me to see them as You do. Help me to consider that maybe they are being used by demonic spirits to attempt to do harm. Help me, Father God.

In the complete name of Jesus, I pray.

Amen.

_____
_____
_____
_____
_____
_____
_____

The Sanctity of Singleness

1 Corinthians 7:1—2

Now for the matters you wrote about: "It is good for a man not to have sexual relations with a woman." ² But since sexual immorality is occurring, each man should have sexual relations with his own wife, and each woman with her own husband.

Lord,

As You give out the instructions for married couples, I am paying close attention. I am trying to decide how to accomplish that level in my marriage. Lord, I will need Your intervention and Your love and Your guidance. I will need direction and Your spirit of peace in order to be the mate that You require and that my mate deserves!

Lord Almighty, may I seek Your face and Your voice when times are troubling and bleak.

May I be sensitive to both Your voice and guidance, as well as to my mate's needs and concerns.

In the awesome name of Jesus, I pray.

Amen.

_____
_____
_____
_____
_____
_____
_____
_____
_____

1 Corinthians 7:8—9

⁸ Now to the unmarried and the widows I say: It is good for them to stay unmarried, as I do. ⁹ But if they cannot control themselves, they should marry, for it is better to marry than to burn with passion.

Dear God,

If only I could remain married and be okay with that. But I cannot seem to be okay with that. I have pleaded and begged for a mate, someone to occupy my time, hold my hand, to argue with, and to love. This 'someone' will even distract me from You. I am probably behaving worse than when Israel begged for a king.

For that, Lord, I apologize. I cannot understand why it is in Your will that I am void of a mate. I cannot see what You see or know. I just want to marry and possibly have children.

Help me survive whatever Your will—either married or single. Whatever Your will, I will praise and follow You.

In the mighty name of Jesus, I pray.

Amen.

The Sanctity of Singleness

1 Corinthians 7:27—28

[27] Are you pledged to a woman? Do not seek to be released. Are you free from such a commitment? Do not look for a wife. [28] But if you do marry, you have not sinned; and if a virgin marries, she has not sinned. But those who marry will face many troubles in this life, and I want to spare you this.

Lord.

I pray to understand the mystery with wisdom of a successful marriage. Lord, I don't know why it is so hard to be married. For such a beautiful collision of two people, I am saddened that this happens to the couples.

Father, I am so surprised that after all of the work and anxiety, money and time that getting married requires that the couple does not give it all that they have to make it work. I am absolutely confused about waiting all this time to get married and not give a real effort to make it work.

What happens God? God, I pray for the health of the marriage for which I prayed. I pray for the strength and courage to sustain that marriage. I pray to work for that which I have prayed.

In the delightful name of Jesus, I pray.

Amen.

Six Months of Solitude

1 Corinthians 7:32—35

³² I would like you to be free from concern. An unmarried man is concerned about the Lord's affairs—how he can please the Lord. ³³ But a married man is concerned about the affairs of this world—how he can please his wife— ³⁴ and his interests are divided.

Lord,

I apologize for my lack of discipline and my desire for divided interests. I am not a good self-disciplinarian. I want what pleases me, and often I do not see that my desire distances me from You.

As a single person, I am supposed to be dedicated to You, but I am not as dedicated as I should be. Lord, I am so sorry that I have not done all that I can for You as a single person.

I don't really even deserve all that I have asked for, but I thought I did because of my mediocrity in service. Please forgive me and help me see and to seize opportunities to do better.

In the promising name of Jesus, I pray.

Amen.

The Sanctity of Singleness

1 Corinthians 7:32—35

An unmarried woman or virgin is concerned about the Lord's affairs: Her aim is to be devoted to the Lord in both body and spirit. But a married woman is concerned about the affairs of this world—how she can please her husband. [35] I am saying this for your own good, not to restrict you, but that you may live in a right way in undivided devotion to the Lord.

Lord,

I know that Your word as it is written is true. I have to believe that my interests will be divided. Correct me if I am wrong, but it seems like You said that I will be choosing my spouse over You. I know that You know me better than I know myself. I so do not want to disappoint You! But according to my historical behavior and Your word, I am destined to disappoint because I will be divided and will most often pick my spouse over You.

Lord, help! I need Your help. Help us to both choose You. Help us to see the reasons and to be compelled to choose You!

In the priceless name of Jesus, I pray.

Amen.

Romans 5:1—2

Therefore, since we have been justified through faith, we have peace with God through our Lord Jesus Christ, ² through whom we have gained access by faith into this grace in which we now stand. And we boast in the hope of the glory of God.

Lord,

I am offered faith because of Jesus' death, burial and resurrection, and His faith. Because of that, You offered me Your peace, which is sometimes beyond my understanding. Now, I stand in Your grace. In addition, You have given me Your hope.

So You did all of that so that I can have faith, peace, grace and hope.

I have more of an idea of faith and the faith that is required to live a life that pleases You.

A peace that restores my self-esteem and keeps me whole.

With grace that helps me offer compassion to others. And hope that keeps me focused on You and You alone.

In the sophisticated name of Jesus, I pray.

Amen.

The Sanctity of Singleness

Romans 5:3—5

³ Not only so, but we also glory in our sufferings, because we know that suffering produces perseverance; ⁴ perseverance, character; and character, hope. ⁵ And hope does not put us to shame, because God's love has been poured out into our hearts through the Holy Spirit, who has been given to us.

Lord,

I have considered what kind of mate I want so I definitely need to figure out what I will be as a mate. I do know that I need to me more consistent when I am suffering, and act the same way I do when life is good.

That suffering should produce perseverance, if I don't quit. Please help me not to quit. That perseverance produces character. Character is who I am when You are watching. I want to have great character. Then hope. I want to be hopeful and optimistic. Hope does not put me to shame. Jesus does not leave me to look foolish, but Christ—like.

I want to persevere, have character, hopeful, and function in Your love.

I love You, Lord.

I pray in the loving name of Jesus.

Amen.

Romans 7:14—20

[14] We know that the law is spiritual; but I am unspiritual, sold as a slave to sin. [15] I do not understand what I do. For what I want to do I do not do, but what I hate I do. [16] And if I do what I do not want to do, I agree that the law is good. [17] As it is, it is no longer I myself who do it, but it is sin living in me.

Lord,

I choose to do wrong often. There are times when I feel bad for doing wrong, then there are times when I don't. I need to access the power which You have stored with me to overcome the enemy. Lord, I apologize for embarrassing You, causing people to question if I am a Christian and what You actually do. For that I apologize.

I need Your help Lord, keep the hedge of protection around me very high. Help me to see the escape of temptation which You provide when temptation comes my way.

Lord, remind me that You are my God and my God alone. I don't need to do wrong to be satisfied or victorious.

In the magnificent name of Jesus, I pray.

Amen.

_____
_____
_____
_____
_____
_____
_____
_____

THE SANCTITY OF SINGLENESS

Romans 7:14—20

[18] For I know that good itself does not dwell in me, that is, in my sinful nature. For I have the desire to do what is good, but I cannot carry it out. [19] For I do not do the good I want to do, but the evil I do not want to do—this I keep on doing. [20] Now if I do what I do not want to do, it is no longer I who do it, but it is sin living in me that does it.

Father,

Help me to be the kind of mate that helps to keep us on track. Help me to remain focused on You as I gain a mate. Help me to remember that You sent my mate and that we were prepared for each either, so we need to treat each other the way You prescribed.

Help me to see the potential pitfalls as I make decisions. Lord, I do not want people to question Your sovereignty because of my behavior, actions and attitude. Lord, help me to avoid sin, and I want to bring You honor and glory and praise.

Also, Lord, help me to respond when I see the escape You provide, so that I remain the child You have chosen to carry out Your will with the mate You have chosen and prepared.

In the special name of Jesus, I pray.

Amen.

Romans 8:18

[18] I consider that our present sufferings are not worth comparing with the glory that will be revealed in us.

Mighty God,

I am working to stop considering my current situation of singleness as suffering. I am not actually suffering. I am alone so that I can grow emotionally and spiritually, remind me of that.

I feel like that I am alone because You are punishing me. While that may not be true but that's how I feel because other people get married when I want to so badly. I do not know that I want You to make this feeling go away, but I wish that I had a mate that will love me like I want to be and deserved to be loved—like I am prepared to love someone else.

I just want someone to share my life with, to pray with, to share my days with, and to love out loud in front of.

In the beautiful of Jesus, I pray.

Amen.

The Sanctity of Singleness

1 Thessalonians 5:17

¹⁷ pray continually

God,

I need to be a mate who prays about everything, all the time. Help me be the prayerful mate, demonstrating my faith and trust in You, God!

May my mate be able to rely on me for all that we need in our prayer life. I want to be sure that we can grow closer to You because of prayer.

Lord, help me to commit to prayer so that I can commit my life, thoughts, dreams, concerns, and all anxiety to You. And my mate and family can do the same.

Jesus showed us how to pray and demonstrated how to pray regularly.

I know that I will not receive all that I pray for, but still pray for all things.

In the prayerful name of Jesus, I pray.

Amen.

_____
_____
_____
_____
_____
_____
_____
_____
_____

1 Corinthians 7:19b

Keeping God's commands is what counts.

Dear God,

I am trying to be obedient and it is so hard! Keeping Your commands is what counts! I am struggling to consistently keep Your commands. Help me to remain in covenant mode as I meet and marry the mate of Your choosing.

Help me mature so that You will not continue to be so disappointed.

Help me to keep Your commands!

I need to keep them. I love You! Sometimes I am selfish.

And not thinking about the consequences of my actions.

In the name of my Lord, and Savior Jesus Christ, I pray.

Amen.

The Sanctity of Singleness

1 Peter 2:9

⁹ But you are a chosen people, a royal priesthood, a holy nation, God's special possession, that you may declare the praises of him who called you out of darkness into his wonderful light.

Yahweh,

I am a chosen people! Thank You for reminding me that I am not junk and not a mistake. You picked me, while others reject me . . . daily. And sometimes that rejection comes from people that You actually assigned to love me.

Father, I don't know how to be a royal priesthood now, but could You teach me, show me what it means to be the chosen one that You need me to be.

And I am definitely not holy on a consistent basis. Please provide Your guidance and counsel. I need it now.

But the best thing is that I am Your special possession. Such that no one else's opinion of me should matter or impact me in such a negative way any longer. Thank You for loving me enough to do all of that.

Thank You for providing me with light and subtracting the darkness I was trying to master.

In the dynamic name of Jesus, I pray.

Amen.

_____
_____
_____
_____
_____

Hebrews 12:14—15

[14] Make every effort to live in peace with everyone and to be holy; without holiness no one will see the Lord. [15] See to it that no one falls short of the grace of God and that no bitter root grows up to cause trouble and defile many.

Lord,

Help me to love with peace, to be peaceful, and to create a peaceful existence so that others can do the same, especially my mate, especially and friends.

There is so much chaos in the world, it is hard to realize peace and harder to love peaceably. It is hard to present peace to others who do not want to be peaceful.

I want peace in my home, heart and spirit. Help me to attain that peace and maintain that life style for myself and my mate.

Help me to be holy and to share Your holiness with others.

Help and remind me to be graceful to others and help others to have grace.

In the kind name of Jesus, I pray.

Amen.

The Sanctity of Singleness

1 Thessalonians 5:12—13

[12] Now we ask you, brothers and sisters, to acknowledge those who work hard among you, who care for you in the Lord and who admonish you. [13] Hold them in the highest regard in love because of their work. Live in peace with each other.

Father God,

Bless those of us with work ethic! I work hard most of the time and I want my work ethic to represent Your will.

Father, I am praying for more people who authentically care about me. I need the ability to discern when people care about me and when they do not.

May I be better at accepting the admonishment of others so that I can love according to Your will.

I do love people who have causes and work with all of their hearts to achieve goals which bring You glory.

I will live in peace and will help others to do the same.

In the peaceful name of Jesus, I pray.

Amen.

_____
_____
_____
_____
_____
_____
_____

1 Thessalonians 5:14

¹⁴ And we urge you, brothers and sisters, warn those who are idle and disruptive, encourage the disheartened, help the weak, be patient with everyone.

Father,

First of all, let me be neither disruptive nor idle, because I know that behavior leads to destruction.

I pray to be an encouragement to the disheartened at all times. I pray for those who are sent to encourage me: that they come, and that I am receptive to their encouragement. May I help the weak at all times. And be compassionate, as well as a blessing to them. Someone was helpful to me when I was weak. I thank You for Your love for me via others. May I do the same. Lord, may I be patient, and patient! And patient!

May the blessings You give me to give to others be delivered on time and openly and willingly.

In the patient name of Jesus, I pray.

Amen.

_____

_____

_____

_____

_____

_____

_____

_____

_____

The Sanctity of Singleness

1 Thessalonians 5:15

[15] Make sure that nobody pays back wrong for wrong, but always strive to do what is good for each other and for everyone else.

Lord,

Help me to not be vengeful, not to take revenge on others, and does not pay back wrong for wrong. Lord, help me to forget what is done to me, so that I do not find myself in a position to violate this command.

Lord, I am so often wronged and I so want to not be wronged anymore. I know that it builds character, but I would like to avoid it in the future. Lord, thank You for giving me a good spirit to be good to others without regard for what I receive in return.

I like it when others are helped and happy.

In the good name of Jesus, I pray.

Amen.

_____

_____

_____

_____

_____

_____

_____

_____

_____

1 Thessalonians 5:16

[16] Rejoice always

Sovereign Lord,

Help me rejoice always, especially when it looks hopeless and bleak.

May I rejoice:

> When there's sun and rain.
> When there's love and criticism.
> When there's joy and disgust.
> When there's grief and gratitude.
> When there's distress and happiness.
> When there's loyalty and betrayal.
> When there's bliss and heartbreak.
> When there's peace and drama.
> Where there's rest and weariness.
> When there's relief and weakness.
> When there's strength and flaws.

In all of that, You are there, God. I need to rejoice always.

In the joyful name of Jesus, I pray.

Amen.

_____
_____
_____
_____
_____
_____
_____
_____

THE SANCTITY OF SINGLENESS

1 Thessalonians 5:18

[18] give thanks in all circumstances; for this is God's will for you in Christ Jesus.

Dear God,

Thankfulness is my duty in life. For all that You do and all that You prevent me from experiencing, which would harm me.

Thank You for Your amazing and unconditional love! The love that keeps me whole, heals my wounds, and fixes my broken heart. I am thankful for Your hand of protection and Your infinite wisdom. And Your will and Your plans for me.

I am thankful for being able to help others. I am grateful that You created me. I am grateful that You have stopped me from death. I am grateful that You are the lifter of my head and the peace keeper. I am grateful that You forgive me and have made me more than a conqueror. Thank You for trusting me.

In the mighty name of Jesus, I pray.

Amen.

_____
_____
_____
_____
_____
_____
_____
_____
_____

1 Thessalonians 5:19

[19] Do not quench the Spirit.

Lord,

May I not be the one who quenches the spirit. I know that I do not always pay attention to Your urgings and the signals that You send so that I can avoid danger and sin.

Lord, I need to be better with understanding You so that I can stop quenching You and the Holy Spirit.

I pray that I will learn how to not quench You.

I pray in the powerful name of Jesus, I ask.

Amen.

The Sanctity of Singleness

1 Thessalonians 5:20—21

[20] Do not treat prophecies with contempt [21] but test them all; hold on to what is good

Dear Father,

Help me treat others and prophecies with love and grace, rather than with contempt and hate.

I am trying to do better about how I treat others and how I judge people, even though I should not. Please help me to always see all that is positive and be able to use that to reach a better place for both of us.

Father, please help me to remember that as Your child I am supposed to love Your other children. Because of that love, I should be able to treat them well, forgive them, encourage them, and to hold on to the good within them.

Help me test those for which I have questions.

In the prophetic name of Jesus, I pray.

Amen.

_____
_____
_____
_____
_____
_____
_____
_____

1 Thessalonians 5:22

²² reject every kind of evil.

Lord,

I am sorry for every time that I was evil to others. I apologize for every time that I was evil to someone that You sent my way to share and witness, but instead I brought embarrassment to Your name. I am ashamed of my evil behavior and I pray that my evilness will not cause anyone to turn away from You or cause someone to question You.

I am committed to change my evil ways and evil intentioned words and deeds, and my evil doings.

Please help me to change my evil ways and to stop being evil to people, especially when they are being evil to me. Help me to not repay evil because of the evil given to me. Help me to get out of Your way when You are fighting my battles.

In the covenant name of Jesus, I pray.

Amen.

_____
_____
_____
_____
_____
_____
_____
_____
_____

The Sanctity of Singleness

Colossians 3:23

²³ Whatever you do, work at it with all your heart, as working for the Lord, not for human masters,

Father God,

May I possess the type of work ethic that influences me to do the work You have sent for me to do and blessed me with to be a part of. Lord, help me to remain courageous in the work ethic especially when the work is hard; especially when I hate the work; especially when I hate the people who I serve.

Help me with working on my life such that my work ethic supports Your mission and purpose. Help me to surrender my heart to my work so that it will please You and I give You the highest effort.

Lord, remind me that my work for You is the only work that will last! So Lord I dedicate my work to You! I dedicate my knowledge to You! I dedicate my desires to You! I commit my work to You and surrender myself to You! In ALL that I do!

Remind me of why You sent me when I got weary or start to complain. It is not because of the people—my work is designed to draw others to You.

In the giving name of Jesus, I pray.

Amen.

_____
_____
_____
_____
_____
_____

Ephesians 6:7—8

⁷ Serve wholeheartedly, as if you were serving the Lord, not people, ⁸ because you know that the Lord will reward each one for whatever good they do, whether they are slave or free.

Father God,

Help me to draw from the recesses of myself when I am tired and weary of well—doing. Help me and lift me when I am not serving You wholeheartedly. Remind me that You are the keeper of me and all that I possess, all that I am, and all that I do. Remind me that everywhere I am, You sent me. You provide for me when I am there, and You are my hedge of protection through it all.

Thank You for promising Your rewards for my work to others, especially when I don't deserve Your rewards because I have embarrassed You with my attitude and mediocre efforts and flimsy excuses.

Thank You for trusting me with the work that I am assigned and to whom I am assigned. Help me with my heart. Remind me of how strong it is.

In the magnificent name of Jesus, I pray.

Amen.

_____
_____
_____
_____
_____
_____
_____

The Sanctity of Singleness

John 14:1

"Do not let your hearts be troubled. You believe in God; believe also in me."

Mighty God,

I need to beg for Your forgiveness for my worrying and my troubled heart. I get sidetracked and that is not of You. Father God, please help me consistently believe in You! Help my belief. My belief has failed at times.

So God please help me with my belief and my attitude toward situations that happen to me and my family. Father, may I continue to have the faith that pleases You and warms Your heart.

Faith is what pleases You! I need to be more faithful and more consistent with that.

Help me keep my heart from worrying so that I can stop disappointing You.

In the loving name of Jesus, I pray.

Amen.

_____

_____

_____

_____

_____

_____

_____

_____

On Assignment By God

The Sanctity of Singleness

Job

Job 1

Father,

When I read the book of Job and his story, I weep. I am sorry for complaining about small issues and petty situations.

When I read the entire book, I had to stop and pray for forgiveness because I was complaining and moaning about the minimum issues that I have experienced.

Father, I am embarrassed that I ask questions like Job does. We are ridiculous about the questions that we ask You.

Thank You for sharing Job's story. It gives me hope and encourages me to remain faithful. His story reminds me that You gave permission for what I go through, because You trust me to remain faithful and surrendered to You.

I love Job because of his steadfastness.

In the gracious name of Jesus, I pray.

Amen.

_____

_____

_____

_____

_____

_____

_____

_____

Saul and Ananias

Acts 9

God,

When You call on us, we are never ready! Lord, when You call me, please help me to answer properly and to respond accordingly. Lord, I thank You for giving me Saul as an example of what You will do to get my attention and what You will do once You have my attention.

Thank You for sharing Anaias with me. His story was priceless because he is the epitome of how we should not act when we are assigned by God to do something. Anaias is what we really do though. Help me to remember to stay focused on what You want me to do. Help me to trust and to be trustworthy.

Lord, respectfully I want to please You, but sometimes I don't want the calling that You have bestowed me with. My lack of vision and selfishness are costing You blessings. And hurting me. Help.

In the truthful name of Jesus, I pray.

Amen.

_____
_____
_____
_____
_____
_____
_____
_____
_____

THE SANCTITY OF SINGLENESS

Jesus

John 3:16

Father,

You did not see fit to change Your mind about sending Your Son. You could have changed Your mind and heart. You gave us Your Son to live to teach us and to die to afford us some undeserved forgiveness. I would not have been able to do that. Thank You for Jesus.

Thank You the lessons of love, forgiveness, peace, acceptance, and faith. Thank You for praying for me. Thank You for teaching me how to pray. Thank You for teaching me to pray for others.

Thank You for loving me, disciplining me, and teaching me. Thank You for saving my sorry soul.

Christ, thank You for carrying my burdens and wiping my tears. Thank You for caring for my soul. Thank You for teaching me how to teach and gifting me to do so. Lord, thank You for showing me how to walk on water. Christ, thank You for Your everyday life, teaching us how to accept and love others as they are.

In the priceless name of Jesus, I pray.

Amen.

_____
_____
_____
_____
_____
_____
_____

Samuel

1 Samuel 1

Dear God,

When You created Hannah in order to create Samuel, You were definitely showing off. I admire Samuel because of his relationship with You. Samuel tried to please You and to listen and to learn. Samuel had some of the best assignments and a few of the worst.

But Lord, You trained him early to hear Your voice and to obey You. And to seek Your will. I know that I need to be more like Samuel. I will work on listening more and studying more and obeying Your Holy Spirit more.

I admire his work and work ethic. He reminds of me when he tries to make sense of Your instructions. I do that all of the time. Help me be more discerning about what which I see, hear, and witness. I need to be ready for the many important assignments You have for me.

In the caring name of Jesus, I pray.

Amen.

_____
_____
_____
_____
_____
_____
_____
_____
_____

The Sanctity of Singleness

Hannah

1 Samuel

Father Almighty,

To be parent like Hannah and Elijah would be an answerer prayer.

Hannah prayed for Your blessing of a child. And she did not quit, whine, complain, or act out. Yet, she persisted in her plea to You, God. Thank You God for using Hannah as an example of what to pray for, how to pray, and how to keep the faith while waiting for an answer.

Hannah is to be admired as a mom and woman. Any woman with some of those qualities is certain to please You and be a great parent to a great man and woman.

May we, my mate and I, be the man and woman that Hannah and Elkanah are. We want to please You and birth a healthy child, live according to Your will and be committed to You.

In the amazing name of Jesus, I pray.

Amen.

John the Baptist

Luke 1:5—25

Sovereign God,

When You blessed Elizabeth with a son, You certainly blessed them.

You sent them John the Baptist. He baptized Jesus, preached the work and spread the Good News of the coming of Jesus.

John the Baptist teaches me to recognize my help and source of all things. I am grateful for him as an example of following a true leader and totally operating in my gifts, especially when it looks bleak.

John reminds me to remain encouraged and focused on what God has assigned to me.

Thank You for showing me John's heart and character. I needed that encouragement.

In the mighty name of Jesus, I pray.

Amen.

_____
_____
_____
_____
_____
_____
_____
_____
_____

The Sanctity of Singleness

Peter

Matthew 14:28—29

God,

Of all of the people in the Bible, Peter teaches some of the most valuable lessons. Peter made some radical decisions—he cut the ear of a soldier off because he was defending Jesus, which Jesus put back, but I have to consider his heart and his lack of wisdom. But Peter is an example for me when I need to risk it all for You.

The most memorable thing that happened was when Peter walks on water. I so envy his walk on water. While I feel like he squandered it, at least he asked to go. Most people would not have even asked.

Jesus prays for Peter. Jesus knows Peter, which means He also knows me. Peter reminds me how difficult it is to be a Christian.

In the forgiving name of Jesus, I pray.

Amen.

_____
_____
_____
_____
_____
_____
_____
_____

Moses

Exodus 34:1—9

Father,

I am glad that I was not chosen to be Moses. Leading those people was the challenge of his life. I might have quit! Well in fact, I do quit when situations seem bleak or if it seems like the outcome will not favor me or be favorable. Further, Moses' sacrifice is an example to us all. He gave his life to the journey from Egypt to the Promised Land. What was supposed to last 11 days, actually lasted 40 years. Lord, I am still trying to figure how that is even possible. But Lord, I regard Your relationship highly because You showed him Yourself, You invested in Moses—You gave him the tablets twice!

Father, You spoke to Moses of Your word, and Your covenant and Your promises. Lord, You loved Moses in a very special way—one which I hope You have for me.

In the special name of Jesus, I pray.

Amen.

_____
_____
_____
_____
_____
_____
_____
_____
_____

THE SANCTITY OF SINGLENESS

Joseph

Genesis 50:20

Mighty God,

You are a keeper! And a planner! And a way-maker! Father, have You used me like this? Have I followed Your plan so that I can help those You send, even the family that discarded me? Lord, I hope that I can be a promoter of some of the most powerful words ever spoken, "You intended to harm me but God intended it for God to accomplish what is now being done, the saving of many lives."

Lord, help me to develop the same attitude as Joseph when people try to harm me and hurt me, and especially when they will need me later. Lord, may I please help me to behave in Your will.

Lord, I love Joseph because of his naïve belief that he can share what You share with him. That reminds me of me. God thank You for Your will that I do not fall at the demise of those who plan for it.

In the prophetic name of Jesus, I pray.

Amen.

Timothy

2 Timothy 1:5

Father God,

Timothy accompanied Paul to serve and he learned what You would have him to do. Lord, I could use a mentor like Paul, but I really want to be an humble servant like Timothy so that I can do Your will.

I want to serve You, so help me to be sensitive to the people You send to me for me to serve. Remind me to be sensitive to the mentor who coaches me to serve. Remind me that I am to also serve my mate. Lord, I am not always giving so help me to remember that if I am following Your will that I am serving others and not keeping count of that service and that sacrifice.

I love You, Lord. Thank You for providing me with the examples I need to grow as a better servant to You.

In the peaceful name of Jesus, I pray.

Amen.

The Sanctity of Singleness

Naomi

Ruth 1:1—15

Lord,

I need a Naomi. Thank You for her wit and wisdom, transparency and leadership. Help us to find 'Naomi's.' And when we find them, remind us to respect her and listen to her, regard her and follow her directions.

I am convinced that the reason that 'Naomi's' do not function in their roles is because there are not any 'Ruth's' functioning in our roles. Help us to better followers, listeners, heeders, and doers of You, Your word and those You send me to follow.

Father, I know that we are smart but often we lack wisdom and to that end, we are not growing as You designed. Please help us.

Lord, make 'Naomi's' sacrifice worth it because I need to grow and grow up.

In the sincere name of Jesus, I pray.

Amen.

_____
_____
_____
_____
_____
_____
_____
_____

David

2 Samuel 5:1—5

Father God,

You sent them a king! A warrior! A servant! A leader! A man after Your own heart! You sent them a man who could pray and has poured out his heart to You in the Psalms. May I have some of that same spirit?! I want to be that servant whom You love and trust. I need to more dependable so that You can trust me. I don't want to disappoint You.

Lord, I just want to be the legacy that You designed. Help me not to fail You, at least not as frequently. I admire David for his patience, obedience, stamina, courage, leadership, perseverance, and his words.

But mostly I admire his heart toward You, God. I pray that I surrender in such a complete way that I am able to win Your heart like David did.

In the name above all names: Jesus, I pray.

Amen.

The Sanctity of Singleness

Nathan

2 Samuel 12:7—12

Master,

No one's job was harder than Nathan. As advisor to David, he had to tell the king that his sins had consequences. What a terrible job and responsibility. Again, Nathan had to be someone You trusted. I want that same trust shared between us. I know I need to work on being trustworthy so that I can be trusted. I have previously done things that would cause You to shake Your head in disappointment at my action or lack thereof.

Father, I want You to look upon me as someone You can depend on for Your will, Your message and Your work. Help me to carry out Your will and work. Help me to be responsible for Your message and to those to whom I am accountable. Nathan was brave and courageous, humble and meek, wise and powerful. You invested in Nathan and You invest in me.

In the responsible name of Jesus, I pray.

Amen.

Esther

Esther 5:1—2

Master,

I was minding my own business just like Esther was when You got my attention. I am still in awe of the amazing things that You do in my life.

I cannot compare my life to that of Esther, but I have experienced some really amazing events and activities in my life. You have answered my prayers and given me some of the desires of my heart.

Lord, what I am asking for now is to be granted the level of companionship that the king and Esther eventually experienced.

Help me to recognize my mate when You send my mate. Esther never anticipated the role of Queen, but the amazing part was the obstacles she overcame in order to arrive at the place which was reserved for God's will.

In the mysterious name of Jesus, I pray.

Amen.

The Sanctity of Singleness

Mary

Luke 1:30—33

Father God,

Pick me, Daddy, Pick Me! I say this when I want something miraculous to me like I see happening to others. But in Mary's case—NO! I am not envious of her being chosen. I guess You knew that too. While I do not want her responsibility, I do want to have as strong a legacy as she has.

I pray to handle what is assigned to me as well as she did. She did not panic or quit, get frustrated or get angry, get upset or sad.

Mary is a great example of how we should receive our gifts and our responsibilities. I hope that I behave in a manner and I hope that I never make You feel like You should have chosen someone else to do what I am assigned.

Lord, I want to please You like Mary did. I want You to be able to count on me to do the miraculous work You have planned for me.

In the miraculous name of Jesus, I pray.

Amen.

_____
_____
_____
_____
_____
_____
_____
_____

Six Months of Solitude

Elizabeth

Luke 1:5—25

Father,

After many years of waiting, I know that she was glad that she was patient. Help me to be patient so that I can receive the ultimate gift, which You have for me.

She didn't get ahead of You—a trait I could use. She didn't complain or whine about her unanswered prayer request—a trait that I could benefit from.

Lord, help me to focus on Your will while I wait.

Lord, what a gift You gave her for waiting and being Your child: John the Baptist, someone who paved the way for Jesus. What trust!

Father, Elizabeth teaches us how to confirm family relationships when she fellowshipped with Mary.

Thank You for her wisdom—her example is still needed.

In the bold name of Jesus, I pray.

Amen.

_____
_____
_____
_____
_____
_____
_____
_____

The Sanctity of Singleness

Noah

Genesis 7

Omnipotent King,

When You assigned Noah to the Ark, he was not quite ready. That was a miraculous task: build an Ark, load his family, and a pair of each animal on the Earth. Lord, Your promise of floods was fulfilled. You wiped the entire Earth clean because of sin. You used Noah to do something so important. Will I ever be used for something as important as that?

Father, help me stay focused on Your assignment because I do not want to fail You. I don't want to embarrass You. I certainly do not want others to judge me based on what I don't do for You.

Father, may I have a family who will help and support me in the endeavors which You have assigned me.

In the positive name of Jesus, I pray.

Amen.

_____
_____
_____
_____
_____
_____
_____
_____

Susanna

Luke 8:3

God,

May I be someone who helps others with my means, without regards to what is in it for me. Help me not to be selfish Please help me to see the needs of others and when I see them, be compelled to immediately help them.

Lord, help me to remember that someone helped me when I was in need.

Help me to remember to be kind and compassionate, loving and giving, the way You commanded me to be. May I be a blessing to everyone that You called on me to bless and make sure I do not miss one opportunity.

Help me to view others with Your lens of love and compassion.

Help me be reminded of my covenant of Christianity.

In the precious name of Jesus, I pray.

Amen.

The Sanctity of Singleness

Lydia

Acts 16:14—15

Mighty God,

Oh to be first! First to accept Jesus as her Lord and Savior. The job that she did to spread Your word. She spread the gospel according to Your word and Your will. We are ever grateful for her diligence and her perseverance.

May I do a fraction of what she did! I cannot seem to invite one person to church or to share You with others. Actually, I do not behave in a way which even leads others to You.

Help me to share You with others without fear of judgement or failure. Help me to not miss any opportunities.

Help me to become sensitive to the timing to invite and share.

In the proud name of Jesus, I pray.

Amen.

_____
_____
_____
_____
_____
_____
_____
_____
_____

Women at the Well

John 4:7—26

Lord,

Help me to be better aware of You in my presence. May I no longer miss Your presence nor Your message.

Keep me from being surprised when You show up and when You send Your representatives to usher me into Your will.

Help me to tell the truth in all things.

May my character grow stronger and more representative of You.

Help me to grow to avoid sin more often and not be so enamored by what sin offers.

Help me to be more righteous and more like You.

In the powerful name of Jesus, I pray.

Amen.

_____
_____
_____
_____
_____
_____
_____
_____
_____

The Sanctity of Singleness

Blind Man

Mark 10:49—51

God,

When You asked him what did he want You to do for him, I could not breathe! Thank You for challenging me to accept Your blessings and Your love. You make me think and consider what I do not consider. Do I want to see? Walk? Talk? Do I want to be made whole? Do I want to? Once I am, will I serve You?

To gain something that either I never had or have not had for a long time certainly grows my appreciation for that missing element.

May I share You with all once I am restored? Help me not to take Your restoration for granted. Help me to help others to be restored and made whole. My example should shine among others so that they can also share Your restorative measures in their lives.

I am grateful to be restored.

In the restorative name of Jesus, I pray.

Amen.

Ruth

Ruth 1:16—18

Father God,

"Where you go, I will follow. Your people will be my people. Your God will be my God." When Ruth said this is Naomi, I was speechless.

Who have I said that to? Who can I say that to? Who can say that to me? How do I know? Have I ever missed any opportunities to hear those words? May I behave such that others will say these words to me.

Please send me someone that will mentor me in that same way.

Father, thank You for You calling on all the mentors and Naomi's. Thank You for all Ruth's and mentees. Continue to bless our attitude as we are approached as a mentor and mentee.

In the personal name of Jesus, I pray.

Amen.

_____
_____
_____
_____
_____
_____
_____
_____
_____

The Sanctity of Singleness

Nehemiah

Nehemiah 1:4—11

Father,

May I be sensitive to the calling on my life. Thank You for showing me favor when I am doing Your will. Lord, help me keep focused as I do Your will. Help me to be courageous as I do the scary parts of Your will.

May others be blessed because I was courageous enough to carry out Your will Your way, even if I am fearful and concerned. Even when I fear failure and because I cannot see the future or the end of the project. Help me to understand the importance of my perseverance during the process, so that I do not quit and so that I give it may all.

May I find favor with the circumstances and conditions which I will endure as I continue to carry out Your will.

In the fearless name of Jesus, I pray.

Amen.

_____
_____
_____
_____
_____
_____
_____
_____

Jeremiah

Jeremiah 1:5; 29:11

Father,

If You had called me to be Jeremiah, then I do not know what You would have me to do.

You used Jeremiah for some of the most powerful words in the Bible.

You told him that You know the plans that You have for us, as if someone had questioned You. You do know what You have planned and what the outcome will be.

Keep me like Jeremiah! Help me to hear You like Jeremiah did. Say the important things to me that You shared with Jeremiah.

Lord, help me to remain upright and blameless before You, so that I can be trusted by You and sought by others.

Thank You for setting me apart.

In the incomparable name of Jesus, I pray.

Amen.

_____
_____
_____
_____
_____
_____
_____
_____

The Sanctity of Singleness

Leper

Matthew 8:1—4

Your Majesty,

I pray to be compassionate to those who would be shunned because skin diseases that can be seen. Help me consider them in a loving manner when meeting their needs and serving them. Help me not to judge them because of their light affliction.

Father, may I be ever grateful that I am not in that same situation. Keep blessing me to bless others, especially those judged by others.

May I continue to be humble about my blessing and continue to be committed to serving You. This is my prayer.

I am grateful that the lepers went to share Your good news after their healing. May they continue for their lifetimes, such that others may share their story.

May I never forget that these afflictions also bring You glory.

In the glorious name of Jesus, I pray.

Amen.

_____
_____
_____
_____
_____
_____
_____
_____

Adulterer Nearly Stoned

John 8:1—11

Father,

When others tried to punish her for her sin, You stepped in and made then consider their own sins such that they walked away, and she lived and was left alone.

My sins are equal to all of the other sin of others—I need to remember that. I need to remember how being judged feels so that I do not.

Father, forgive me for judging others. I definitely do not need to judge anyone and I have done so will that I am above Your punishment and wrath.

I need to be grateful for Your forgiveness and mercy, Your love and compassion on my sorry self. Thank You for saving me, especially for myself. Father, thank You for not holding my sins against me forever.

In the saving name of Jesus, I pray.

Amen.

The Sanctity of Singleness

Thomas

John 20:24—31

Sovereign Father,

I thank You for the faith I have. I do ask for an increase of that faith. I beg Your forgiveness when I have had not only the disbelief, but also the nerve to question and then debate the matter! I hope my 'Thomas' antics are rare.

Help my faith and the communication thereof so that I may help the faith of others. Also, help me faith so that others who I do not even know are watching are helped without me saying a word. As my faith increases, remind me to be more responsible for my behavior: words and deeds. Help me remember that others are watching my faith—my faith is on display. Help me to remember that others EXPECT me to be faithful at all times. I do not get a break.

In the faithful name of Jesus, I pray.

Amen.

Crippled

John 5:1—15

Father God,

Thank You God for Your healing! For myself and for all others, thank You for seeing our afflictions and needs and healing us.

Thank You for making me well. Thank You for making me whole.

Thanks for Your command that I stop making excuses and just get up and walk. Making me well brings You glory. Making me well enhances Your ministry through me.

Help me stay focused on You and my assignment. I pray that I do not complain about my affliction. I pray that peace prevails. I consider the healing an investment for Your future plans.

I continue to pray for favor and grace, love and compassion.

I promise to give You the glory.

In the healing name of Jesus, I pray.

Amen.

_____
_____
_____
_____
_____
_____
_____
_____

THE SANCTITY OF SINGLENESS

The Widow and Elijah

1 Kings 17:7—16

Father God,

Help me to better recognize opportunities to serve You. Help me to see how my service benefits You. The widow is not any different from us. We question You, God, with our actions, even though we may not ask directly.

The widow could only see what was present rather than what her future held. She is just like me. I trust what only I see and my vision is quite limited. So please forgive me for not trusting where You send me. I know that I should trust that everything is by Your design. Even satan has to ask to disrupt Your plans.

Thank You for turning my little flour and my small amount of oil into many meals for my family—way more than I anticipated.

In the visionary name of Jesus, I pray.

Amen.

_____
_____
_____
_____
_____
_____
_____
_____

Six Months of Solitude

Joseph

Matthew 1:18—25

Sovereign Majesty,

You selected Joseph to be Mary's husband. No one knows why Joseph was able to serve in that role. But he wasn't initially clear either. This is an issue for most of the pregnancy. It is not surprising that he was not happy about this situation. However, at some point Joseph's faith and vision matured and the light was shining. Joseph offers us some wisdom in this matter.

Father, thank You for showing me how to respond when something super natural, beyond reality and completely powerful happens out of the blue and makes us question all that we know as true and real.

Help me believe in Your plan, Your will and Your way.

In the insightful name of Jesus, I pray.

Amen.

_____
_____
_____
_____
_____
_____
_____
_____

The Sanctity of Singleness

Zechariah

Luke 1:5—25

Sovereign Lord,

May the wisdom given to Zechariah be given to all. I pray that I never have to be silenced so that I can hear from You and to be obedient. I know certain circumstances can be overwhelming and supernatural, but please help me keep my wits about me so that I do not embarrass You or myself.

Help to bridle my tongue so that I do not use it foolishly. I believe that while I do not how I would have responded, I am praying not to question You or Your messengers. I do not want to disappoint You. I certainly do have questions but I cannot afford to be offensive or silenced. I love You Lord. I do not understand much of what You do. Most is unbelievable as well.

Help me to trust You in all circumstances and believe You for the resolve.

In the gracious name of Jesus, I pray.

Amen.

_____
_____
_____
_____
_____
_____
_____
_____
_____

The Prodigal Son

Luke 15:11-32

Father,

May You continue to bless my family and I. I need help with family management. The hardest detail to consider is how I make them feel when I hold them accountable and tell them how I feel.

Help me to recognize the talents, value and contribution of each family member. Help me try to understand their point of view before I judge or criticize.

Help me to overcome my own self—esteem issues and insecurities so that I can celebrate the accomplishments of others. Help me to be the definition of love as the definition so that I am not envious or prideful, vengeful, or vindictive; so that I am kind and truthful, humble, and do not keep track of wrong doing.

Let me and my family be the model of love so that others will know that it is possible.

In the loving name of Jesus, I pray.

Amen.

_____
_____
_____
_____
_____
_____
_____
_____

The Sanctity of Singleness

Singleness —What To Do While Single

The Sanctity of Singleness

Ephesians 6:11

¹¹ Put on the full armor of God, so that you can take your stand against the devil's schemes.

Mighty God,

Forgive me for leaving the armor at home on a regular basis. I need the armor. I respect Your provision of protection of me. Father, I apologize for not taking that protection more seriously. And stop neglecting it.

Remind me—compel me—to wear the armor. Help me to wear the armor. Most importantly, God help me to put the armor to good use.

Lord, I need the armor which I keep putting down and leaving because the devil is after me and I need a defense against his schemes. Except God, I leave it and yet I beg for Your rescue and assistance.

Again, Lord, I beg Your forgiveness and ask Your compassion on my sorry self.

In the protective name of Jesus, I pray.

Amen.

_____

_____

_____

_____

_____

_____

_____

_____

Ephesians 6:12

[12] For our struggle is not against flesh and blood, but against the rulers, against the authorities, against the powers of this dark world and against the spiritual forces of evil in the heavenly realms

Your Sovereignty,

Of all that You have shown me and shared with me, this is the hardest element to remember and to remember to recognize.

Mighty God, when You revealed to me that the people who I had labeled as my enemy were really only people who were being used by the devil and the dark spiritual forces.

Lord, help me to remember to look past the person to the force behind those evil deeds.

Help me to forgive those who are used by those horrible powers of the dark world.

"My struggle is not against flesh and blood." My battle is not against my family, nor my mate, not my friends, not my co-workers, but the spiritual forces which attempt to use them. Lord, I forgive them because they know not what they do.

In the prayerful name of Jesus, I pray.

Amen.

The Sanctity of Singleness

Ephesians 6:13

¹³ Therefore put on the full armor of God, so that when the day of evil comes, you may be able to stand your ground, and after you have done everything, to stand.

God,

I will use the armor better, God, more often, and correctly and consistently.

The best lesson God was when you showed me that I was already prepared for the attacks which were staged against me. Then You taught me that You did not miss anything and You are handling all of that, without my participation.

God, thank You for reminding me that the day of the evil one will come. I need to be on watch. Lord, when You said stand, I was confused. But later You will reveal how You want me to stand. Am I quiet during this season? Or aggressive? Or combative? Or loving? Or fierce?

Whatever You ask me to do, Lord, I'll do it. And be grateful?

In the awesome name of Jesus, I pray.

Amen.

_____

_____

_____

_____

_____

_____

_____

_____

_____

Ephesians 6:14

. ⁱ⁴ Stand firm then, with the belt of truth buckled around your waist, with the breastplate of righteousness in place,

Lord,

Sometimes I waver and I should not. Help me Lord, to stand firm. I need Your help. Rather than standing firm, I yield to sin, accept the devil's invitation to deter others from being Your children, and to doubt.

Lord, I need help remembering what You have for me to do and who You called and gifted me to be. I need Your help!

I am buckling the belt of truth around my waist and I pray to never take it off. Help me to be honest and to also accept the truth as You share it.

Lord, my breast plate of righteousness is fitted and in place so that I can reject the enemy's schemes, I hope it never comes off because I resist the urge for it come off.

In the perfect name of Jesus, I pray.

Amen.

_____
_____
_____
_____
_____
_____
_____
_____
_____

The Sanctity of Singleness

Ephesians 6:15

¹⁵ and with your feet fitted with the readiness that comes from the gospel of peace.

Father God,

You are patient and merciful. I love You so much. May my feet be ever ready for Your assignment and the work that You have for me.

Thank You for Your provision of the armor! You have made provision for me even when I do not know that I need Your protection.

The Gospel of Peace is my source for all that I do not know. Lord, help me to read more, understand more, and share more.

The Gospel of Peace—Your Holy Word—provides me with some peace and comfort and a lot of instructions. Please help me to read Your word more and to apply it more and more consistently. Father, help me to be brave when I am challenged by the opportunity to chose against You.

Father, help me to share Your word with others.

In the obedient name of Jesus, I pray.

Amen.

Ephesians 6:16

¹⁶ In addition to all this, take up the shield of faith, with which you can extinguish all the flaming arrows of the evil one.

God,

I am not faithful and I should with my shield of faith. Again, You have provided me with protection but I have neglected it. I need that shield which I do not seem to have with me at all times. I don't even know how or where I put it down. And when I do need it, I don't actually reach for it. I beg You for it. Lord, please forgive me for my neglectful and nuisance behavior.

Father, forgive me for not being faithful to You as I should.

Help me to be more faithful! Help me to be more committed to You.

Keep me accountable to You for the life that pleases You—only with faith.

In the faithful name of Jesus, I pray.

Amen.

THE SANCTITY OF SINGLENESS

Ephesians 6:17

¹⁷ Take the helmet of salvation and the sword of the Spirit, which is the word of God.

Sovereign God,

The armor requires focus on You and a commitment to You which is unwavering and characteristic of the Christian You have called me to be.

I promise to put the helmet of salvation on. And to never remove it. My salvation and that of others are at risk daily; even hourly—at every minute and every second. If I am wearing my helmet and when I help others wear theirs as well, then the risk is lessened. Even eliminated.

I promise to use the Sword of the Spirit—the word of God—so that I can have a better understanding of You. Help me to understand it. Help me to share. Help me to understand how to teach others to do so as well.

I yearn for Your favor and blessings over my life. I promise to stop neglecting my tools—Your provision! The answer to earlier prayers—all of them.

In the promising name of Jesus, I pray.

Amen.

_____
_____
_____
_____
_____
_____
_____
_____

Ephesians 6:18

¹⁸ And pray in the Spirit on all occasions with all kinds of prayers and requests. With this in mind, be alert and always keep on praying for all the Lord's people.

My Father,

Help me to pray. Help me to pray more and more each day. Help me to pray for all things. Help me to submit my total self to You through prayer. Help me to pray for others according to their needs and Your will.

Lord, help me to share everything because I know that I keep certain information and issues to myself, when I am supposed to share them with You.

Father, help me to remain alert. Help me to see the world around me and to get invested in it so that I can do Your work and Your will.

Help me to be sensitive to the Holy Spirit when He directs me to pray.

In the praying name of Jesus, I pray.

Amen.

_____

_____

_____

_____

_____

_____

_____

_____

The Sanctity of Singleness

Ephesians 6:19—20

[19] Pray also for me, that whenever I speak, words may be given me so that I will fearlessly make known the mystery of the gospel, [20] for which I am an ambassador in chains. Pray that I may declare it fearlessly, as I should.

Father,

I will pray for all messengers for You, including myself. I need help when I speak because sometimes I lack 'salt' and tact when I share information with others. For that, I am truly apologetic. Help me to remember that others depend on me to pray. You send them to me to pray, but I have been neglectful before. I am sorry for the times that I have been neglectful of other's needs and their prayer concerns.

Father, help me to be sensitive as I pray for others that I keep their issues confidential and I treat them with compassion and love.

I cannot say that I know of Your mysteries or that of the gospel to be an expert or authority, but I will share what I want to do know.

Please help me to let others pray for me.

In the prayerful name of Jesus, I pray.

Amen.

Ephesians 5:1—2

[1] Follow God's example, therefore, as dearly loved children [2] and walk in the way of love, just as Christ loved us and gave himself up for us as a fragrant offering and sacrifice to God.

God,

Jesus has such a romantic and wonderful love of me, of us. His love is so awesome and wonderful and unduplicatable.

When You gave Jesus the gift to love, we were not ready to receive it or to share it. We were not ready to receive it or to share it. I have been affected by the cruelness of this world, which rejects love, and all who love.

Thank You for Jesus and His example of love. Thank You for helping me to love more. Thank You for helping me to love more, to love in a healthier way. Thank You for teaching me how to love in an authentic manner.

Thank You for helping me to share love selflessly and compassionately, fearlessly and without anxiety.

I love You, God and Jesus. And Holy Spirit.

In the loving name of Jesus, I pray.

Amen.

_____
_____
_____
_____
_____
_____
_____

The Sanctity of Singleness

Ephesians 5:3

³ But among you there must not be even a hint of sexual immorality, or of any kind of impurity, or of greed, because these are improper for God's holy people.

Father God,

I need to beg Your forgiveness for all that I do that is improper for God's Holy people. Lord, I want to stop doing the immoral, the impure, and the greedy behavior that I have done. Forgive me for poorly influencing others; who sin based on something that I have done or not done. Lord, help me to overcome the urge to sin and the temptation to sin regardless of my personal thoughts. Lord, help me to recognize the escape You have provided for me to not sin. I want to recognize the escape so that I escape the sin, sin that so easily entangles me. Sin that makes You wish that I would pay more attention. God, you expect me to measure, enhance, embrace, and share him. I have grown in Your ways, will, and word.

In the forgiving name of Jesus, I pray.

Amen.

_____
_____
_____
_____
_____
_____
_____
_____
_____
_____

Ephesians 5:4

⁴ Nor should there be obscenity, foolish talk or coarse joking, which are out of place, but rather thanksgiving.

Father,

We are attacked daily with the words of others, including our authoritative figures, including our parents, elected officials and our teachers.

Help us disregard these examples and those who share that example of that I do not fall victim to the sin which follows.

Help clean up my mind and mouth so the perception and actual behavior transitions from 'it was me' to with certainty that 'it was not me and I would never.'

Help me find other ways, more productive and non-offensive ways, to express my anger and displeasure for issues which arise which usually stimulate this poor behavior and choice of words. Lord, I apologize for embarrassing You.

In the perfect name of Jesus, I pray.

Amen.

_____

_____

_____

_____

_____

_____

_____

_____

The Sanctity of Singleness

Ephesians 5:5

⁵ For of this you can be sure: No immoral, impure or greedy person—such a person is an idolater—has any inheritance in the kingdom of Christ and of God.

Father God,

I want Your inheritance more than anything ever! I know that I disappoint You daily. I pray that I disappoint You less and less everyday. I do want my testimony to include Your inheritance and favor, blessings and grace, love and forgiveness, mercy and power.

May I please You with my effort toward You and others. May I please You with my attitude about You and Your will. May I please You with my faith. May I please You with my service. May I please You with my love for others. May I please You with my effort to follow Your will. I pray that I can be sensitive to Your voice, Your worship, Your unctions, and Your will.

I pray that You are pleased with me trying to be the person You intended for me to be.

In the strong name of Jesus, I pray.

Amen.

_____
_____
_____
_____
_____
_____
_____

Six Months of Solitude

Ephesians 5:6—7

⁶ Let no one deceive you with empty words, for because of such things God's wrath comes on those who are disobedient. ⁷ Therefore do not be partners with them.

Father,

May my words not be empty! May I speak truth and wholesome talk to everyone that I meet, regardless of how they make me feel, and what I actually want to say.

May I be on watch and on guard for those who try to deceive me with their words. I pray that I am on alert with all that happens around me, so that the devil's schemes will not overtake me or change my focus!

I hope I am spared Your wrath for my disobedience. I hope I never get what I deserve. I pray that You forgive me and do not subject me to Your wrath, which I deserve, but would never survive. Help me keep careful watch over the company that I keep.

In the compassionate name of Jesus, I pray.

Amen.

_____

_____

_____

_____

_____

_____

_____

_____

The Sanctity of Singleness

Ephesians 5:8—9

⁸ For you were once darkness, but now you are light in the Lord. Live as children of light ⁹ (for the fruit of the light consists in all goodness, righteousness and truth)

Father,

There is a distant difference between light and darkness, good and evil, good and bod. I am light. Thank You God for making me light! Thank You making me good. Thank You for reclaiming me when I got close to darkness, evil and bad. Lord, I remember flirting with the darkness, but of course, I never thought I would be pulled in; never thought it would be longer than today. When You sent that messenger, I ignored them. I am now clear that it was horrible idea. When You sent that message to stay away, I did not heed Your warning. This was the worse decision I have ever made.

Help me to be good. I need to be good. Help me to be courageous enough to be righteous. Righteous is not popular but it is necessary. Help me to live with and share truth. Help me to be bold enough to do all of that You command and expect.

In the righteous name of Jesus, I pray.

Amen.

Ephesians 5:10

¹⁰ and find out what pleases the Lord.

Lord,

I need to know how to please You, God. I need to know what is acceptable to You. Then I need to do ONLY that. Lord, I spend so much time trying to please myself that I do not seek Your face regarding any matters. I do not ask Your approval when I pursue my desires. Help me to understand what You want, what is acceptable to You.

Help me keep focused on what is acceptable. Help me to be obedient when You tell me no regarding my desires, essentially when my desires contradict Your will.

Help me to crave doing Your will with my talents and offering You my talents in Your will.

In the willing name of Jesus, I pray.

Amen.

THE SANCTITY OF SINGLENESS

Ephesians 5:11

[11] Have nothing to do with the fruitless deeds of darkness, but rather expose them.

Father,

I want: help—Your help—in overcoming darkness and being darkness. Please help me to see the darkness. Please help me turn away from the darkness. Please help me around the darkness and the evil that it harbors and shelters.

Father, most importantly help me to not be darkness—the evil which hurts others and sometimes causes them to turn away from You and to question You.

Father, help guide my focus and order my steps when You send me to expose darkness and wrong doing. Help me to remain calm when I am exposed to darkness. Help me to remember to act in love because they are just being used by spirits. Help me to seek Your solutions even in this situation.

In the name of light of Himself, Jesus Christ, I pray.

Amen.

Ephesians 3:16—17a

[16] I pray that out of his glorious riches he may strengthen you with power through his Spirit in your inner being, [17] so that Christ may dwell in your hearts through faith.

Lord,

How I thank You and love You! Please help me to access the strength that You provide for me. Lord, I know that You have given me strength but I cannot seem to access it when I need it. Please stir it within me such that I am able to use that inner strength to overcome my various obstacles and issues.

Lord, I thank You for the existence of Christ and the Holy Spirit. I thank You for their indwelling within me, in my heart with faith.

Help me to continue to have the faith which pleases You.

Help me to mobilize my faith so that as I do Your work and Your will that I will not doubt nor will I quit.

In the strong name of Jesus, I pray.

Amen.

_____
_____
_____
_____
_____
_____
_____
_____

THE SANCTITY OF SINGLENESS

Ephesians 3:17—18

And I pray that you, being rooted and established in love, [18] may have power, together with all the Lord's holy people, to grasp how wide and long and high and deep is the love of Christ,

Father,

Thank You for Paul, his ministry, and especially his prayers for me.

Thank You for rooting and establishing me in love—especially Your love! I do not realize it in my times of despair but You love me and I was conceived and birthed out of love! Thank You!

Father, thank You for power that You have given me to understand Your measure of love and Your definition of love. Your love is high and wide and deep and long. Your love is infinite and all encompassing. Your love includes me. It defines me. It defends me. It created me. It deepens my understanding of Your word. Your love is profound. Your love is exciting. Your love is my stronghold. Your love! Your love is amazing! Your infinite love is my foundation. It is the way that You keep me alive.

In the loving name of Jesus, I pray.

Amen.

_____
_____
_____
_____
_____
_____
_____
_____

Ephesians 6:19

¹⁹ and to know this love that surpasses knowledge—that you may be filled to the measure of all the fullness of God.

Dear Father God,

I do not understand Your love and I don't need to understand it. Your love does not need my understanding to cover my sins, revive my spirit, restore my love, and provide my protection. Your love lifts my head and dries my eyes. Your love holds me close and keeps me safe.

Your love keeps me sane and helps me grow. Your love defines how I love others and how I forgive them as well. Your love reminds me of my identity when others would like to bully me and hurt me. Your love keeps me whole and restrains me when I am not obedient or compliant.

Thank You for loving me! Thank You, Lord, for loving me extravagantly and while I do not deserve it.

In the loving name of Jesus, I pray.

Amen.

The Sanctity of Singleness

John 14:21

²¹ Whoever has my commands and keeps them is the one who loves me. The one who loves me will be loved by my Father, and I too will love them and show myself to them."

God,

I know that You can measure my love by my obedience. I love You and I try to be obedient. I will strive daily to keep Your commands; some days are easier than others.

I love You, Jesus. I know that You love me God. I am certainly undeserving.

Jesus, thank You for showing Yourself to me. Jesus, thank You for saving me from myself. Thank You for my life and my protection. Sometimes, Jesus I am not aware of what You save me from or keep me away from or who You keep away from me.

Thank You for all that I do see, but especially all that I do not!

Father, thank You!

In the protective name of Jesus, I pray.

Amen.

John 13:14

¹⁴ Now that I, your Lord and Teacher, have washed your feet, you also should wash one another's feet.

Father God,

When I read this scripture, I weep. Jesus, I consider the foot washing a life—long lesson of service. Jesus, You washed the disciples feet! Jesus, You wash my feet when You teach me to live for You, to love You, to love others, to be obedient, and to be whole.

Father, please help me understand how to share what You taught me with others. I want others to understand how to serve others.

Help me to meet others to teach and to serve. Help me to serve others who do not know You and do not understand You and Your saving power and Your abundant love.

It was more than about the feet—it was about my life. You made me a better person.

In the whole name of Jesus, I pray.

Amen.

_____

_____

_____

_____

_____

_____

_____

_____

The Sanctity of Singleness

Ephesians 1:15—16

¹⁵ For this reason, ever since I heard about your faith in the Lord Jesus and your love for all God's people, ¹⁶ I have not stopped giving thanks for you, remembering you in my prayers.

Father,

Paul is such an example. I hope that I represent You the way that he does. Paul prays for me. I know that I need to pray for others more. I need to pray for them in their presence and alone. I do not pray enough.

Lord, I pray that my reputation for my love for others and my faith in You is strong enough for someone to say what Paul said to the Ephesians.

I want my love for others—all God's people—to show up in everything that I do. Please help me!

I am still in need of help with my faith. I want my faith to be seen by others as an example to all that are watching to be drawn to You.

In the faithful name of Jesus, I pray.

Amen.

_____

_____

_____

_____

_____

_____

_____

_____

Luke 9:23—25

²³ Then he said to them all: "Whoever wants to be my disciple must deny themselves and take up their cross daily and follow me. ²⁴ For whoever wants to save their life will lose it, but whoever loses their life for me will save it. ²⁵ What good is it for someone to gain the whole world, and yet lose or forfeit their very self?

Oh Lord,

May I realize when You expect me to deny myself. I desire to come after You! I desire to follow You! I desire to be known as Your disciple and Your representative.

I hope and pray that my disappointment will be limited. I pray that my missteps are not detrimental to others who are following You or are trying to follow You. I am so sorry for all of the trouble I have caused others who try to serve You. I apologize for serving You inconsistently.

Help me deny myself—I cannot seem to do it alone. Help me to stop trying to save myself and my life in my times of distress; especially when I am trying to avoid You and Your discipline.

Lord, thank You for reminding me that some gains in this world will deter me from You—keep me from that fatal mistake. I don't want to forfeit my soul.

In the life—giving name of Jesus, I pray.

Amen.

_____
_____
_____
_____
_____

The Sanctity of Singleness

Matthew 25:14—30

²⁴ "Then the man who had received one bag of gold came. 'Master,' he said, 'I knew that you are a hard man, harvesting where you have not sown and gathering where you have not scattered seed. ²⁵ So I was afraid and went out and hid your gold in the ground. See, here is what belongs to you.'
²⁶ "His master replied, 'You wicked, lazy servant! So you knew that I harvest where I have not sown and gather where I have not scattered seed? ²⁷ Well then, you should have put my money on deposit with the bankers, so that when I returned I would have received it back with interest.

Lord,

When I hear this story, I have to think over my life and my gifts, ensuring that I am not sacrificing a gift by not using it. Help me to use each gift as You have designed it to be. May I continue to share my gifts and employ them to bring others to the kingdom of God.

I pray that I do not use them to the selfishness of my personal service and personal benefit. May I share my gifts so that others may grow and flourish.

Lord, help my attitude be gracious and representative of Your will and Your way. Help me to help others make good use of their gifts as well.

Father, may I be productive with my gifts to bring glory and honor to Your name! I want that abundance You promised in Your word. I want to be available to be used by Your and all that service entails.

In the giving name of Jesus, I pray.

Amen.

_____

_____

_____

_____

Luke 15:8—10

⁸ "Or suppose a woman has ten silver coins[a] and loses one. Doesn't she light a lamp, sweep the house and search carefully until she finds it? ⁹ And when she finds it, she calls her friends and neighbors together and says, 'Rejoice with me; I have found my lost coin.' ¹⁰ In the same way, I tell you, there is rejoicing in the presence of the angels of God over one sinner who repents."

Father God,

May I be ever conscious of what You have blessed me with, so much so that I never take not one element for granted. Never let me take one lost piece of silver for granted. Lord, remind me to imitate the lady and her lost piece of silver. Help me pay attention with a special love and detail for everyone that crosses my path, such that everyone will have a relationship with You, Father. You saved me. I will help in saving them, too. When I was lost, You searched for me and sent for me. When I wandered away from Your protection and guidance, You sent for me and found me. You brought me back. Help me to help others to return to You the way that I did.

The angels rejoiced and I am grateful! I will seek, search, and find others who have lost their way. I will also rejoice upon their return.

In the compassionate name of Jesus, I pray.

Amen.

_____

_____

_____

_____

_____

_____

THE SANCTITY OF SINGLENESS

Matthew 4:1—11

Then Jesus was led by the Spirit into the wilderness to be tempted by the devil. ² After fasting forty days and forty nights, he was hungry. ³ The tempter came to him and said, "If you are the Son of God, tell these stones to become bread."

Father,

Tests! You give them. I take them—some I pass and others, I fail. Some last longer than others, and most of the time, I don't know how long these tests will last.

But Jesus was tested for 40 days. He knew that He was going to be tested. He knew that He had to pass the tests. He knew that He could not quit. I want to quit and my assignment is not nearly as important as Yours. I want to quit when it is easy, and especially when it is hard.

Lord, thank You for being an example for me to persevere and to overcome the light afflictions. Lord, thank You for teaching me to survive the tests. Thank You for making them survivable. Thank You for making me strong enough to be Your child.

In the strong name of Jesus, I pray.

Amen.

Matthew 26:36—46

³⁹ Going a little farther, he fell with his face to the ground and prayed, "My Father, if it is possible, may this cup be taken from me. Yet not as I will, but as you will."
⁴⁰ Then he returned to his disciples and found them sleeping. "Couldn't you men keep watch with me for one hour?" he asked Peter. ⁴¹ "Watch and pray so that you will not fall into temptation. The spirit is willing, but the flesh is weak."

Dear Father God,

May the lessons Jesus taught at Gethsemane live on with me forever more! Father, thank You for teaching me to persevere when adversity is in my path. Thank You for helping me to be accountable for my prayer life, helping me to understand what is important and how that translates into my daily walk as Your child. Thank You for sharing with me how important it is when You say no.

Father, thank You for sharing with me how to submit and surrender to Your will regardless of what it will cost me.

Lord, I felt compassion for Jesus when I read this prayer about the cup. I know how it feels to want to be excused from certain callings and responsibilities. I know how it be told no.

Thank You for sharing the why, the how, and the outcome with me— You certainly do not owe me an explanation.

In the transparent name of Jesus, I pray.

Amen.

_____
_____
_____
_____
_____

THE SANCTITY OF SINGLENESS

Isaiah 55:8—9

⁸ "For my thoughts are not your thoughts,
   neither are your ways my ways,"
declares the LORD.
⁹ "As the heavens are higher than the earth,
   so are my ways higher than your ways
   and my thoughts than your thoughts.

Father God,

These verses are some of the most amazing scriptures in the Bible. Thank You for that. God, You have shared with me Your decrees, Your laws, Your will, Your way, Your calling on my life, and the gifts that You have bestowed upon me!

Thank You for making sure that I understood our differences. It gives me an elevated understanding and an extraordinary hope about what You have planned for me.

Father, I am overwhelmed with these verses because I am relieved that You are a planned God and this is a great statement and realization.

Lord, thank You for Your thoughts and Your ways toward me.

Thank You, God.

In the thoughtful name of Jesus, I pray.

Amen.

_____
_____
_____
_____
_____
_____

Matthew 28:19—20

[19] Therefore go and make disciples of all nations, baptizing them in the name of the Father and of the Son and of the Holy Spirit, [20] and teaching them to obey everything I have commanded you. And surely I am with you always, to the very end of the age."

Father God,

May I pay attention to the signs of those I need to so that I do not miss an opportunity to share You with others. I know that I have missed some opportunities and ignored others, and for that I apologize.

I pray to be alert at all times so that I do not miss anyone You send my way.

I promise to help them to be disciples—teaching them to teach and helping them to pray. Just like someone did for me.

I will teach baptism and will help them understand the importance and the non—negotiability of the process. I promise to teach them all that You have taught me—all that I have learned! That is a lot. Thank You for teaching me and allowing me through trust to teach others.

Thank You for being with me until the end of the age—the end of time. I love You and I adore You.

In the adoring name of Jesus, I pray.

Amen.

_____
_____
_____
_____
_____
_____
_____

The Sanctity of Singleness

Reflections

Reflections

Appendix

My Testimony	229
Prayer Directions	232
Prayer Request List/Journal	233
Marriage Covenant	237
Marriage Vows	239
Resources	243

The Sanctity of Singleness

My Testimony

My testimony is my experience with God and the results of that experience. This includes my first encounter with Christ to my current life.

Consider the answers to the following questions to develop your testimony:

1. When did I first meet Christ?
2. How do I share how I met Christ with others?
3. What have my encounters with God been like?
4. What is my relationship with God like?
5. What danger has He kept me from?
6. What have I done that would have sabotaged God's work if He had not stopped me?
7. What has happened that I realized that only God was in charge to make this happen?

_____
_____
_____
_____
_____
_____
_____
_____
_____
_____

The Sanctity of Singleness

Prayer
A Short How To Guide

The prayers which are most effective follow the following "rules:"

- It is a conversation with God.
- Be Honest with God.
- This is a relationship.
- God is to be praised, worshiped and glorified.
- God likes His word prayed back to Him.
- This is not a list of stuff I want.
- Think of more than myself when you pray.
- Be authentic with God and myself.
- Be prepared for people to ask me about my prayer life and faith.
- Do not worry about big words or long sentences.
- Please know that God is not taking revenge on others for me, and vice versa.
- Please prayer in the name of Jesus.
- There is no correct way to pray.

Scriptures on Prayer

Matthew 6:9-14

1 Thessalonians 5:17

Matthew 26:

John 17

Prayer Requests
Prayer Journal

1. What am I asking God for?
2. What am I hoping God will do?
3. What am I expecting from God?
4. What has God already done to exceed my expectations?
5. What has God done to get my attention?
6. What has He shown about Himself and me?

THE SANCTITY OF SINGLENESS

Six Months of Solitude

The Sanctity of Singleness

Marriage Covenant

The Sanctity of Singleness

Marriage Vows

The Sanctity of Singleness

Six Months of Solitude

The Sanctity of Singleness

Resources

www.onediagage.com

As We Grow Together Daily Devotional for Expectant Couples

As We Grow Together Prayer Journal for Expectant Couples

As We Grow Together: Workbook for Expectant Couples Her Workbook

As We Grow Together: Workbook for Expectant Couples His Workbook

The Best 40 Days of Your Life: A Journey of Spiritual Renewal

The Blue Print: Poetry for the Soul

From Fat to Fit in 90 Days: A Fitness Journal

From Two to One: The Notebook for the Christian Couple

Hannah's Voice: Powerful Lessons in Prayer

Her Story: The Legacy of Her Fight The Devotional

Her Story: The Legacy of Her Fight The Legacy Journal

Her Story: The Legacy of Her Fight Prayers and Journal

In Her Own Words: Notebook for the Christian Woman

In Purple Ink: Poetry for the Spirit

The Intensive Retreat for Couples for Her

The Intensive Retreat for Couples for Him

The Measure of a Woman: The Details of Her Soul

One Day More Than We Deserve Prayer Journal for the Growing Christian

Promises, Promises: A Christian Novel

Six Months of Solitude: The Sanctity of Singleness Devotional

Tools for These Times: Timely Sermons for Uncertain Times

With An Anointed Voice: The Power of Prayer

The Sanctity of Singleness

Yielded and Submitted: A Woman's Journey for a Life Dedicated to God

Yielded and Submitted: A Woman's Journey for a Life Dedicated to God Intimate Study

Yielded and Submitted: A Woman's Journey for a Life Dedicated to God Prayers and Journal

The Power of a Praying Woman Stormie Omartian

The Power of a Praying Wife Stormie Omartian

The Power of a Praying Husband Stormie Omartian

Discerning the Voice of God Priscilla Shrirer

Kingdom Woman Tony Evans and Crystal Evans Hurst

Kingdom Man Tony Evans

I Kissed Dating Goodbye Joshua Harris

The Five Love Languages for Singles Dr. Gary Chapman

Love and Respect Dr. Emerson Eggerichs

Friends, Lovers and Soul Mates Drs. Derek and Darlene Hopson

Saving Your Marriage Before It Starts Drs. Parrot

Saving Your Second Marriage Before It Starts Drs. Parrot

The Excellent Wife Martha Peace

Knight and Shining Armor P B. Wilson

When God Writes Your Love Story Eric and Leslie Ludy

The Four Seasons of Marriage Dr. Gary Chapman

The Love Dare Stephen and Alex Kendrick

Faith Tango Carolyn and Craig Williford

War Room Chris Farby

Acknowledgements

God, thank You for Your plans for me. Thank You for ***Six Months of Solitude: The Sanctity of Singleness Prayers and Journal*** and choosing me to complete Your project. I just want to please You. Thank You for continuing to anoint me and to invest in me and my gifts, which keep surprising me. Thank You for loving and forgiving me.

Damita Phillips, thank you for reading my work and offering your feedback. I know that you had to laugh and struggle through the reading of it.

Hillary and Nehemiah, thank you for supporting me and my endeavors. Thank you for loving me, especially when I do nothing without a pen and a clipboard, thank you for enduring my late nights, your ideas, the sounding board, the love and the support. Thank you for celebrating our legacy.

To my prayer partners and to my accountability partners, thank you for the long talks and the powerful prayers and the encouragement. To my pastor and church family, thank you so much for your love and support.

Minister Onedia N. Gage seeks to share her outlandish pursuit of God with her prayers, study and meditation. She desires to share her faith in a manner which helps you do the same through her calling. She hopes that these words bless you.

Please feel free to contact and share your testimony. onediagage@onediagage.com, or @onediangage (twitter). www.onediagage.com

Blogtalkradio.com/onediagage

Youtube.com/onediagage

Facebook.com/onedia-gage-ministries

The Sanctity of Singleness

Preacher ♦ Advocate ♦ Teacher ♦ Facilitator

Conference Speaker ♦ Workshop Leader

To invite Rev. Gage to speak to the young adults and Single's Ministry at your church, women's ministry,

The full congregation or any other ministry.

Please contact us at: www.onedigage.com

@onediangage (twitter) ♦ onediagage@onediagage.com ♦ facebook.com/onediagageministries

youtube.com/onediagage ♦ blogtalkradio.com/onediagage ♦ ongage (Instagram)

THE SANCTITY OF SINGLENESS

Publishing

Do you have a book you want to write, but do not know what to do?

Do you have a book you need to publish but do not know how to start?

Would publishing move your career forward?

Let us help

onediagage@purpleink.net ♦ www.purpleink.net

281.740.5143 ♦ 713.705.5530